DIVINE HEALING

THE CHILDREN'S BREAD

DIVINE HEALING

The
Children's
Bread

BY

KEITH M. BAILEY

CHRISTIAN PUBLICATIONS
Camp Hill, Pennsylvania

Christian Publications
3825 Hartzdale Drive, Camp Hill, PA 17011

Faithful, biblical publishing—since 1883

ISBN: 0-87509-233-0
LOC Catalog Card Number: 77-83941
© 1977 by Christian Publications
All rights reserved
Printed in the United States of America

94 95 96 97 98   8 7 6 5 4

Unless otherwise indicated, Scripture taken from the
New American Standard Bible,© The Lockman Foundation
1960, 1962, 1963, 1968, 1971, 1972, 1973, 1975, 1977.

Cover Design by
Robert A. Baddorf

Contents

	Foreword	7
1	The Children's Bread	9
2	Distinguishing the Two Aspects of Healing ..	27
3	Healing and the Atonement	43
4	Healing in Early Biblical History...........	59
5	The Period of the Kings and Prophets	75
6	The Healing Christ	97
7	The Healing Church	113
8	The Gifts of Healings....................	143
9	Divine Healing and Demon Possession......	157
10	Divine Healing and Modern Medicine.......	177
11	Healing and the Faith Factor	187
12	Divine Healing in the Ancient Church	199
13	The Modern Healing Movement	211

Contents

Foreword

The pressures and conflicts in the closing years of the twentieth century have made the message of the gospel of Christ more necessary than ever before. It must meet the needs of men spiritually, intellectually, and physically by offering answers to the problems posed by a changing civilization and by the increasing needs for the stamina to maintain the exhausting pace of modern living. The daily emergencies of life demand a whole gospel for the whole man.

Dr. Bailey has attempted in this book to present a survey of the teaching on God's provision for human health and healing as given in the Bible and as practiced in the historic Christian church. His coverage is comprehensive, his attitude both positive and irenic, and his teaching understandable. He makes no extravagant claims and neither underrates nor exaggerates the importance of his subject. Aspects peculiarly pertinent to modern interests are the discussion of the relation of divine healing to the work of physicians, and also to the recent rise of interest in occult practices.

This presentation of healing is free from any connotation of fanaticism or of propaganda. It is not advocating showmanship or miracle-mongering. Rather, it contends that healing is an integral aspect of Christian experience, resulting from the intervention of God, who rescues His children from the ravages of disease in order that they may serve Him more effectively. The author has studied his subject carefully and has written from the perspective of a ministry in which healing has constituted a valid and recognizable part.

Merrill C. Tenney
Wheaton College
Wheaton, Illinois

1

The Children's Bread

And Jesus went away from there, and withdrew into the district of Tyre and Sidon. And behold, a Canaanite woman came out from that region, and began to cry out, saying, "Have mercy on me, O Lord, Son of David; my daughter is cruelly demon-possessed." But He did not answer her a word. And His disciples came to Him and kept asking Him, saying, "Send her away, for she is shouting out after us." But He answered and said, "I was sent only to the lost sheep of the house of Israel." But she came and began to bow down before Him, saying, "Lord, help me!" And He answered and said, "It is not good to take the children's bread and throw it to the dogs." But she said, "Yes, Lord; but even the dogs feed on the crumbs which fall from their master's table." Then Jesus answered and said to her, "O woman, your faith is great; be it done for you as you wish." And her daughter was healed at once (Matt. 15:21-28).

THE CANAANITE WOMAN was from a pagan community and background. Matthew's account of her encounter with Jesus reveals she had knowledge of the faith of Israel. She addresses Him as "Son of David" and acknowledges Him as the providing Lord both of Israel and of her own people.

Jesus' answer to the troubled woman offers an important insight to bodily healing when He calls it "the children's bread." He was implying no racial or ethnic discrimination in His answer. Rather, He wanted her to know that the blessing of physical healing by divine intervention was the unique privilege of a covenant people in proper relationship to God and that He had come as the Messiah of Israel to fulfill the covenant with them.

> *Is anyone among you sick? Let him call for the elders of the church, and let them pray over him, anointing him with oil in the name of the Lord; and the prayer offered in faith will restore the one who is sick, and the Lord will raise him up, and if he has committed sins, they will be forgiven him. Therefore, confess your sins to one another, and pray for one another, so that you may be healed. The effective prayer of a righteous man can accomplish much* (James 5:14-16).

Instruction for the ministry of healing as taught in the Epistles is depicted in the context of the local church and becomes "gifts of healing" in the ministries of the Christian assembly (1 Cor. 12:9, 30). Healings, described as "wonders and signs," did occur during mass meetings and on public occasions (Acts 2:43; 5:12; 14:3). But the positive expectation for healing is presented as being for the children who have entered the family and household of God, and it is these who have been given this special provision.

The importance of healing in today's church

The Christian church after centuries of neglect is again giving serious attention to its responsibilities to "heal the sick" (Matt. 10:8; see James 5:16). Christian healing is not only a live issue today, but also an issue that is relevant to the needs of twentieth-century people. This generation's cry for help, stemming from physical and mental suffering, reveals that the need for healing has not been abated with the advancement of medical science and, therefore, cannot be ignored by the church.

More and more it is recognized that biochemistry, surgery, modern medicine, and psychiatry fail to touch the interfusion between man's physical and spiritual needs. New advances reveal new complications often related to a dimension in man's need that modern medicine is not prepared to serve.

Modern man is almost obsessed with matters of health. He has daily exposure through the media to the latest developments of medicine. Books and magazines on health problems, nutrition, prevention of illness, and every other aspect of health enjoy increasing popularity.

With this interest has come a new interest in the occult and the hope it may be a source of healing power. The trend in modern theology toward a secular gospel has developed a vacuum for the occult so that with the advancement of so-called scientific progress has come a widespread renewal of interest in various forms of spiritual healing.

There has been an increase in the skill levels of hospital workers. Specialists unknown previously, like inhalation therapists, have entered the field. New equipment for renal dialysis and nuclear scanning, for example, has been added. This has resulted in prohibitive costs for the average citizen with a demand for more adequate health protection. National health insurance programs along with overcrowded hospitals and doctors' offices are inevitable.

But with all this burden man's health problems have created, the spiritual need of man is increasingly being displaced. The effectiveness of the church's ministry is being dissipated as it tends to adjust to the world's false dichotomy between body and spirit. Man has been divided, his wholeness neglected.

The need for a theology of healing in the church

Every Christian clergyman and layman should seek a working knowledge of what the Bible has to say about bodily healing. Every assembly of believers seeking to be truly New Testament in doctrine and practice should offer a healing ministry in its total church program.

Christian healing relates to the whole body of Christian truth. The cults and quacks practice a spurious kind of healing, resting on principles of sorcery, spiritism, and, in some cases, downright deception. The Christian healing ministry of the church stands on a completely different foundation.

True Christian healing in both concept and method has come to man by way of divine revelation and is set apart from other forms of spiritual healing in that it has a theology. The revealed Word of God and the incarnate Christ stand in perfect harmony in behalf of the whole man. Though Christianity, in the long run, makes technology possible in terms of its view of an ordered universe, it alone can protect man from an arbitrary exploitation of his physical needs.

Proponents of modern theology with its mysticism—based on existential philosophy—have encouraged separation of man's spiritual nature from his physical nature. Many evangelicals have avoided a theology of physical healing as part of the theology of redemption. They tend to relegate physical healing to a creational design and thus refer it onesidedly to a theology of creation.

The biblical view is *re*demption, *re*generation, and God's fulfillment of His purpose for man on the basis of the original creation. The two, creation and redemption (including Christ as Creator-Redeemer), must be held together to avoid perverted views that both exploit and neglect man's physical needs. The believer cannot routinely make his way to the house of worship at the hour of prayer and fail to minister to the lame man at the gate. Alms alone are not adequate to meet man's needs if we believe the full implications of an incarnate, resurrected, living Lord who is the same yesterday, today, and forever.

The redemptive concept of healing

The world is sick and has been from the first hour that it was infected by sin. The news commentator who called America a "sick society" the day President Kennedy was assassinated had not come up with a new idea. Whether he was aware of it or not, he only echoed the prophet Isaiah, who said of the social order in his day,

> *Alas, sinful nation,*
> *People weighed down with iniquity,*
> *Offspring of evildoers,*
> *Sons who act corruptly!*

> *The whole head is sick,*
> *And the whole heart is faint.*
> *From the sole of the foot even to the head*
> *There is nothing sound in it.*
> *Only bruises, welts, and raw wounds,*
> *Not pressed out or bandaged,*
> *Not softened with oil* (Isa. 1:4a, 5b-6).

Twentieth-century men cry with ancient Israel, "Is there no balm in Gilead? Is there no physician there?" The Bible shouts back, "Yes, there is a physician. The Redeemer Jesus Christ, the Son of God, has healing in His wings."

Sickness is the fruit of human depravity

When men are ready to admit that their sickness is the fruit of human depravity, the Bible answer will have meaning. Redemptive healing pours like a stream from the wounds of Christ for every sickness of man's spirit, soul, and body. To those who believe the healing balm will come.

The last reference to healing in the Bible refers to this healing stream.

> *And he showed me a river of the water of life, clear as crystal, coming from the throne of God and of the Lamb, in the middle of its street. And on either side of the river was the tree of life, bearing twelve kinds of fruit, yielding its fruit every month; and the leaves of the tree were for the healing of the nations* (Rev. 22:1-2).

The context leads to the conclusion that this scene describes conditions in the eternal age. A similar passage is Ezekiel 47:12:

> *"And by the river on its bank, on one side and on the other, will grow all kinds of trees for food. Their leaves will not wither, and their fruit will not fail. They will bear every month because their water flows from the sanctuary, and their fruit will be for food and their leaves for healing."*

The prophetic vision of Ezekiel has its setting in the land of Israel and no doubt pictures the blessing of the kingdom age.

The key to John's vision goes back farther than Ezekiel's prophecy. It goes back to Eden and the original state of man. While Adam lived in Paradise he had access to the tree of life. Man was forbidden to eat of the tree of the knowledge of good and evil lest he die. Satan challenged the death warning, implying that man's independence from God held additional benefits that God was deliberately withholding, and tempted man to disobey the Creator.

Adam's fall required his removal from the garden "lest he stretch out his hand, and take also from the tree of life, and eat, and live forever" (Gen. 3:22). This removal was evidently an act of mercy lest Adam should be confirmed irrevocably and immortally in a state of sin. Cherubim, with the flaming sword, were stationed to "guard the way to the tree of life" (Gen. 3:24).

Jesus Christ, by His death and resurrection, has opened a new access to His provisions. When His redemptive work has accomplished its end, redeemed man will taste the health-giving leaves of the tree of life once again. The gospel invitation is to return to life as provided in Christ. The life of the Redeemer as represented by the tree of life is for the whole man. Ultimately, the healing of redemption is intended to restore man to the full benefits of that life. The leaves speak figuratively of blessing (Ezek. 47:12; Rev. 22:2) and prosperity (Ps. 1:3) beyond essential needs for daily living. And though the mortal believer does not live in a garden of paradise isolated from a sin-cursed world, he does have the life of Christ—life that is manifest for the benefit of spirit, soul, and body.

The relationship of sickness to sin

There is no evidence in Scripture that disease and infirmity were an essential part of man's existence prior to the fall. The presence of sickness in human existence today may be attributed to sin's invasion of the human race. Adam had no need for healing in the garden.

Unfortunately, some Bible teachers have not been careful to distinguish between this remote cause of sickness in mankind as a whole and the immediate cause of sickness in an individual today. While they are related they are not the same.

The apostle Paul makes clear that man is presently under a profusion of futility and a slavery of corruption that for the believer inspire hope for a final and complete deliverance:

> *For the creation was subjected to futility, not of its own will, but because of Him who subjected it, in hope that the creation itself also will be set free from its slavery to corruption into the freedom of the glory of the children of God. For we know that the whole creation groans and suffers the pains of childbirth together until now. And not only this, but also we ourselves, having the first fruits of the Spirit, even we ourselves groan within ourselves, waiting eagerly for our adoption as sons, the redemption of our body* (Rom. 8:20-23).

Because of this situation, and because of our present weaknesses, intercession in prayer demands recognition of the Holy Spirit's guidance in the light of God's ultimate purpose for those who love God:

> *But if we hope for what we do not see, with perseverance we wait eagerly for it.*
>
> *And in the same way the Spirit also helps our weakness; for we do not know how to pray as we should, but the Spirit Himself intercedes for us with groanings too deep for words; and He who searches the hearts knows what the mind of the Spirit is, because He intercedes for the saints according to the will of God.*

> *And we know that God causes all things to work together for good to those who love God, to those who are called according to His purpose* (Rom. 8:25-28).

Prayer for physical healing does not mean that the believer is to be free from all creaturely futility, corruption, and weakness. It does mean that he has access to the throne whereby he may be brought into divine alignment with the purpose of God and be consciously assured that things are working together for good.

Romans 8:28 is not the language of acquiescence and passive acceptance, but the language of challenge to inherit the provision of life and blessing included in God's purposes despite the situation incurred by the fall.

Paul, in listing elements of futility and corruption in the context of Romans 8, names tribulation, distress, persecution, famine, nakedness, peril, and sword as those elements that challenge the believer's faith in the love of God. "But," he says, "in all these things we overwhelmingly conquer through Him who loved us" (Rom. 8:37).

Evidently, *in all these things* believers share a common bond of suffering with unbelievers. However, the believer has a resource to live victoriously in the midst of such circumstances. Sickness is not one of them. Though the argument from silence is not conclusive, it may well indicate that God never intended the believer to suffer sickness in common bond with unbelievers, as in the elements listed.

In any case, the general conclusion to be drawn is that sickness is an effect of sin in the human family. As such, its ultimate defeat must be by the redemption of Christ.

The redemptive factor in relation to sickness

The first teaching on healing that God gave to His people suggests that in the mind of God physical healing was a redemptive matter. The children of Israel had been delivered from Egyptian bondage and were enroute to the land of promise.

The relationship they sustained to Jehovah was secured and maintained by a blood covenant. It was when the paschal lamb was slain and the blood applied that Israel was delivered from the bondage of Egypt. At the waters of Marah God chose to reveal Israel's heritage. At the appropriate time the people of Israel were made to face the first crisis of their position as a people totally dependent upon God. It is plainly to be a covenantal benefit available to them through the redemptive name *Jehovah-rapha*, meaning "I, the Lord, am your healer" (Ex. 15:26).

> *And when they came to Marah, they could not drink the waters of Marah, for they were bitter; therefore it was named Marah. So the people grumbled at Moses, saying, "What shall we drink?" Then he cried out to the Lord, and the Lord showed him a tree; and he threw it into the waters, and the waters became sweet. There He made for them a statute and regulation, and there He tested them. And He said, "If you will give earnest heed to the voice of the Lord your God, and do what is right in His sight, and give ear to His commandments, and keep all His statutes, I will put none of the diseases on you which I have put on the Egyptians; for I, the Lord, am your healer"* (Ezek. 15:23-26).

There are records of healing prior to Israel's experience at Marah, but it was there that the people of God were first offered a healing promise. Upon meeting the conditions laid down by Jehovah, they could expect both the prevention of disease and the healing of infirmities.

These blessings for their physical bodies formed an integral part of the redemption they had received through the shed blood of the paschal lamb and on the basis of their covenantal relationship to Jehovah.

The place of healing in the covenant is further verified by the revelation given to Moses on Mount Sinai—a remarkable healing provision:

> *But you shall serve the Lord your God, and He will bless your bread and your water; and I will remove sickness from your midst* (Exod. 23:25).

Jehovah's promise to Israel rested on the conditions of keeping the terms of the covenant.

The Lord revealed to Moses the possibility of His inflicting the curse of disease upon His people in the event of their willful disobedience to the divine covenant (Lev. 26:16; Deut. 28:27-28, 35). Spiritual laws, then, affect physical illness. This very fact argues in favor of a redemptive aspect in divine healing.

During the wilderness journey the time came when God judged the covenant people severely for rebelling against His anointed servants Moses and Aaron. The full account is given in Numbers 16:41-50.

A plague sent from God killed 14,700 people in the camp of Israel. The Lord summoned Moses and Aaron before Him and ordered an atonement to be made to stop the devastation of this divinely imposed epidemic of disease. Aaron, acting as intercessor, ran into the midst of the people and made an atonement. By this means alone was the plague stopped. Whatever typical meaning one may choose to give to this passage does not alter the objective fact that physical deliverance came by the means of atonement.

The association of bodily healing with redemption seems consistent in the experience of ancient Israel. Numbers 21:4-9 tells of a divine retribution upon the people for their unjust criticism of Moses. Poisonous snakes invaded the camp, causing scores of people to die. Scripture indicates that the victims lived only a short time after being bitten. By divine revelation Moses was instructed to make a serpent of bronze metal and fasten it on a pole placed in a conspicuous place among the people. From the moment a victim of a snake bite looked on the pole he was instantly healed of the ordinarily fatal physical effects of the bite.

Reference to this incident was made by Christ as He talked with Nicodemus:

> *And as Moses lifted up the serpent in the wilderness, even so must the Son of Man be lifted up; that whoever believes may in Him have eternal life* (John 3:14-15).

The brazen serpent is a type of Christ crucified. If a fatal physical condition was healed through this type of the cross, is it unreasonable to assume that healing has a relationship to the cross?

Before leaving the writings of Moses, there is a passage in Leviticus, chapters thirteen and fourteen, that is relevant to the subject of bodily healing and redemption. These chapters detail the laws required for the cleansing of a leper. The symptoms described in chapter thirteen indicate that the disease under discussion was different from the leprosy prevalent in Asia in modern times. It appears to have been even more dreadful.

A person contracting leprosy in the camp of Israel was by priestly action declared ceremonially unclean and was required to live outside the camp, cut off from the worship of the tabernacle. Some see in chapter fourteen a means of healing the leper, but this is not the case. The priest was to visit the leper to determine whether or not he had been healed of the disease (Lev. 14:3). If healing had already taken place, a sin offering, trespass offering, and burnt offering were made. The function, then, of the offerings was the removal of the leper's ceremonial condition of uncleanness.

However, there is no warrant to conclude that this passage has no bearing on the teaching of healing in the atonement. J. H. Oerter comments on this chapter:

> By an expiatory and substitutional sacrifice he is restored again to fellowship with God and His people. But at the same time his healing and cleansing are not considered complete and actual until those atoning sacrifices have been made for him. A full physical as well as a levitical and theocratical cleansing and restoration is perfected only by means of an atonement.[1]

Since the leper's state of uncleanness was the direct result of his disease, it seems to imply a relationship between his physical and spiritual conditions. Atonement was necessary to full restoration. The law of the cleansing of the leper certainly contributes to the viewpoint that for the ancient covenant people bodily healing was a redemptive matter.

The Old Testament saints understood this truth and learned the benefit of its appropriation by faith. The psalmist breaks into song at the thought of his own experience of healing:

> *Bless the Lord, O my soul;*
> *And all that is within me, bless His holy name.*
> *Bless the Lord, O my soul,*
> *And forget none of His benefits;*
> *Who pardons all your iniquities;*
> *Who heals all your diseases;*
> *Who redeems your life from the pit;*
> *Who crowns you with lovingkindness and compassion*
>   (Ps. 103:1-4).

Many commentators have interpreted the phrase *who redeems your life from the pit (destruction,* KJ) as having reference *only* to deliverance from the pit. *Redeem,* then, would have a future application to bodily resurrection. But the use of the present indicates that the writer had in mind a present application of Jehovah's power.

Albert Barnes, Presbyterian minister and author of a commentary on the New Testament, expands the possibilities of meaning in this verse by suggesting that in view of the context the psalmist meant that Jehovah saves the believer from death when the body is exposed to great danger and when the body is attacked by disease.[2]

Whether or not one accepts Barnes' conclusion, it does seem obvious from the Psalm that its author believed bodily healing to be redemptive. He saw it in the same stream of divine favor that granted him the forgiveness of sin.

The Old Testament Scriptures by covenant, historical record, type, and prophecy present the healing of the body as an integral part of redemption. The Matthew passage brings this truth into clear focus by demonstrating that the doctrine of healing in the New Testament has its roots in the doctrine of healing known to Israel in the Old Testament.

The Greek New Testament contributes to the idea of healing as a redemptional issue. The common verb for *save* in the Greek New Testament, *sōzō,* is used to express the direct and immediate application of Christ's redemptive power to the believing sinner. This same verb used consistently to express salvation of the soul is used also in seventeen New Testament passages, to express physical healing. Such usage seems to infer that the inspired writers saw healing as related to salvation. They were not forced to this usage by the poverty of the language, for the Greek language has more than one word for healing.

The root idea of *sōzō* is to make "safe and sound." The salvation of man is to make him safe and sound in every part of his personality. The very employment of this word suggests that the interest of salvation is the whole man. It is not possible in the biblical scheme to isolate the body and have salvation apply exclusively to man's higher nature. Christ ultimately saves all of the man, and the benefits of salvation including physical healing may be sought now.

In Romans 8:23, Paul speaks of the "redemption of our body." The body is saved and figures very largely in the interests of redemption. Romans 12:1 calls for the total dedication of the body. First Thessalonians 5:27 states that New Testament salvation sanctified the body on the same level with the soul and the spirit. Numerous passages confirm the doctrine of the resurrection of the body.

The place of the human body in Christian theology is discussed by Paul in his first letter to the Corinthians, chapter six:

> Yet the body is not for immorality, but for the Lord; and the Lord is for the body. Now God has not only raised the Lord, but will also raise us up through His power. Do you not know that your bodies are members of Christ? Shall I then take away the members of Christ and make them members of a harlot? May it never be!
>
> Or do you not know that your body is a temple of the Holy Spirit who is in you, whom you have from God, and that you are not your own? For you have been bought with a price: therefore glorify God in your body (vv. 13b-15, 19-20).

More than bodily resurrection is under consideration in the above verses. Paul teaches that there is a present relationship of the Christian's body to Jesus Christ. The Corinthians had some philosophical hangups about the body, and Paul made it clear that the body counted with Christ.

According to biblical psychology, the body is significant. The inspired writers had defined the total-man conception a full millennium before modern behavioral sciences formulated it. The spirit, soul, and body of a man are so interrelated as to make him a whole being and salvation involves the whole person.

Christians are aware of the future benefit of bodily resurrection, but too few understand the present redemptive benefit the body can enjoy. The body is a member of Christ and the sanctuary of the Holy Spirit. The dedicated body of a Christian has the ability to glorify God in the present life.

One must conclude from this evidence that Paul's summary statement *the body is . . . for the Lord; and the Lord is for the body* contains much neglected truth. That the Redeemer should manifest such interest in the bodies of the saints as this passage describes and yet, as some conclude, have no concern for the health of their bodies seems absurd. Certainly the phrase *the Lord is for the body* means much more than healing, but it seems reasonable that physical healing is a part of that which Christ provides for the body of His child.

The relationship of divine healing to the
whole of Christian experience

An interest in physical healing was common to the nations of the ancient world. In most instances it had religious connotations. Healing, although associated with the supernatural, was void of any true spiritual understanding. Magic and superstition prevailed in even the most advanced cultures.

Israel, God's covenant nation, stood alone in possessing a redemptive doctrine of healing. God's people learned by divine revelation of both healing of the body and healing of the soul. Consideration of this broader redemptive healing as contained in the Scriptures is essential to the study of the truth of physical healing.

J. R. Pridie has urged the need to relate Christian healing for the body, or "spiritual healing" as he calls it, to the whole of Christian experience:

> In considering the subject of spiritual Healing, it is of the greatest importance that we should first see the background of the picture. A great disservice is done when we so far isolate Spiritual Healing from the rest of Christian experience that it seems to stand by itself.[3]

The church's ministry of healing to the physical body becomes an integral part of the whole work of redemption. Physical healing gets out of focus when considered apart from this larger redemptive conception.

---

[1] J. H. Oerter, *Divine Healing in the Light of Scripture,* p. 43.

[2] Albert Barnes, *Notes on the Old Testament: Psalms,* 2:75.

[3] J. R. Pridie, *The Church's Ministry of Healing,* p. 1.

2

Distinguishing the
Two Aspects of Healing

BEFORE THE THEOLOGY of healing is explored in the historical development of progressive revelation, a basic distinction in Scripture will help to clarify many problems that have been raised in conservative evangelical circles.

Discernible distinctions are essential to the understanding of any subject. The distinction between Christian healings as "the children's bread" and divine healing as "signs and wonders" has profound implications.

Christian healing as "the children's bread"

By viewing the phenomena of healing as exclusively a certification of the supernatural, the true stance of the scriptural doctrine of Christian healing is largely lost. Some Bible scholars insist that healing is not healing unless it is a miracle accompanied by a sign.

Many of the recorded incidents of healing were sign-miracles, but most biblical teaching on divine healing is related to the common privilege of the believer. It is "the children's bread." God's people are the principal recipients of His healing touch, and the "gospel loaf" is for those who sit at Christ's table.

From Genesis to Revelation, the record shows that physical healing by divine intervention has been the common experience of the children of God. From the historical viewpoint, incidents of healing were not restricted to unusual times of miraculous manifestation. Even during the so-called silent periods of biblical history, when the open manifestation of the supernatural seems to have been withdrawn, the healing promises remained and the person whose believing heart reached out to God on the ground of promise received His healing touch.

The Scriptures record not only cases of individual and group healings but also a large body of doctrinal truth about healing. The definitions, the governing principles, and the logical implications laid down in the Word of God make healing an ongoing part of God's redemptive dealings with man. There would be no reason for a theology of healing if the sole purpose of the phenomena were the sovereign demonstration of divine power. The doctrine of healing and health is woven into the scriptural view of man.

W. C. Stevens expresses it well:

> Healing by Jesus Christ was no new thing at His advent in human form. It was an essential part of "the bread of God" in former times.[1]

"The children's bread" was more than physical healing since all the blessings of redemption make up this "bread." Unfortunately, many believers do not know that a very real part of the "bread of God" to be eaten by faith is the healing of the body.

The eternal Christ healed throughout the centuries of

Old Testament history. The earliest references to healing are related exclusively to believers, as were most of the healings in the Old Testament.

With the advent of Christ, "the children's bread" became available to those of every tribe and nation who would receive it by faith. Christ conveyed to the Canaanite woman of Tyre that His blessings were not bestowed as products of a peddler on any who sought for them (see Matt. 15:22-28); the phrase *children's bread* implies that He had in mind benefits restricted to believers. The word *children* suggests relationship, and the true believer is a child of God who enjoys a conscious relationship with his heavenly Father.

The New Testament Epistles are not silent on the subject of healing. The emphasis is placed not upon the phenomenon of physical deliverance but rather upon the relationship of bodily health to the total man. Healing as the believer's privilege is discussed in that portion of the Word of God addressed to the church.

As will be demonstrated more fully, the emphasis of the biblical message of physical healing is not on the spectacular public display of miracles but on the day-by-day experience of drawing from Christ the Healer for the needs of the body. Believers will experience fresh newness as they learn to claim by faith the Lord for the body.

Divine healing as "signs and wonders"

Sign miracles are acts to demonstrate God's power and to confirm the gospel; they accomplish His sovereign purpose. These are an exception to the principle of Christian healing as "children's bread."

Mark, who records Jesus as saying, "These signs will accompany those who have believed: . . ." (16:17a), closes his Gospel with this sequel:

So then, when the Lord Jesus had spoken to them, He was received up into heaven, and sat down at the right hand of God. And they went out and preached everywhere, while the Lord worked with them, and confirmed the word by the signs that followed (vv. 19-20).

For almost a century these verses have been under fire from the higher critics. However, the evidence is in favor of their integrity, and the author takes the position that these words are part of the inspired Scriptures. Mark's version of our Lord's Great Commission (Mark 16:15-18) is consistent with the subsequent experiences of the primitive church.

The book of Acts demonstrates the apostolic faith in Jesus' promise and its parallel significance to Jesus' own ministry on earth. On the day of Pentecost, Peter said:

"Men of Israel, listen to these words: Jesus the Nazarene, a man attested to you by God with miracles and wonders and signs which God performed through Him in your midst, just as you yourselves know— . . ." (Acts 2:22).

After Peter's sermon, "everyone kept feeling a sense of awe; and many wonders and signs were taking place through the apostles" (Acts 2:43). The healing of the lame man at the gate (chap. 3) drew a crowd. Peter, using the occasion to preach, said:

"And on the basis of faith in His name, it is the name of Jesus which has strengthened this man whom you see and know; and the faith which comes through Him has given him this perfect health in the presence of you all" (v. 16).

Because a great number of conversions followed, Peter

and John were put into prison, but the church gathered for prayer. At their trial the council noted their confidence "and began to recognize them as having been with Jesus" (4:13). Surely, this meant a very recent audience with the blessed Son of God! Then as the council saw the man who had been healed standing there, they had nothing to say.

After being released with threats Peter and John "went to their own companions, and reported all that the chief priests and elders had said to them" (v. 23). Having heard the report, the gathered believers joined in praise to God and petitioned the living Jesus of Nazareth with these words:

> *"And now, Lord, take note of their threats, and grant that Thy bond-servants may speak Thy word with all confidence, while Thou dost extend Thy hand to heal, and signs and wonders take place through the name of Thy holy Servant Jesus"* (vv. 29-30).

Several times God confirmed His word by miracles, signs, and wonders (8:13; 14:3). Paul wrote to the Romans:

> *For I will not presume to speak of anything except what Christ has accomplished through me, resulting in the obedience of the Gentiles by word and deed, in the power of signs and wonders, in the power of the Spirit; so that from Jerusalem and round about as far as Illyricum I have fully preached the gospel of Christ* (Rom. 15:18-19).

And to the Corinthians:

> *I have become foolish; you yourselves compelled me. Actually I should have been commended by you, for in no respect was I inferior to the most eminent apostles, even though I am a nobody. The signs of a true apostle were performed among you with all persever-ance, by signs and wonders and miracles* (2 Cor. 12:11-12).

From the days of the apostles to the present countless sign-miracles of healing have occurred, particularly where the gospel of Christ has been introduced for the first time. It is not uncommon for the unconverted to be healed of bodily ills. This was true during Christ's earthly ministry and also during the days of the apostles as recorded in the book of Acts. Of those who received healing from the touch of Christ only a small number were saved from sin and persisted in discipleship.

The occurrence of healing as a sign in pagan countries seems to be under the sovereign direction of the Holy Spirit. Such healings often take place to the surprise of the ministers involved.

John Nevius, the renowned Presbyterian missionary to China, found that healings were common among the national Christians at the close of the nineteenth century. Through his extensive studies of the subject of demon possession, Dr. Nevius learned that successful prayer for the sick was far more common than he had thought. Healings were often the means of convincing pagans of the reality of the gospel of Jesus Christ. The national church leaders had received no teaching on this subject. The outbreak of healing seemed to be spontaneous, apart from any doctrinal influence.[2]

Some of the most unusual examples of healing have occurred in denominations that either do not teach or do not lay emphasis on the doctrine of divine intervention in sickness. Marie Monsen, a Norwegian Lutheran missionary, writes of an experience in Shantung, China, in the Southern Baptist Mission during the great revival of 1929.

> There was a clever but very proud Chinese doctor who had been the subject of our prayers for a long time. He had two patients who were very seriously ill and had been bedridden for twenty years. He said he would be saved if they were

healed. The Christians accepted the challenge and met to pray for them. Both patients were healed within two days of each other. The doctor was also saved, and so delivered from pride that he became a humble witness for the Lord; and from that time on was often to be found in the poorest homes.[3]

During the first two decades of the twentieth century remarkable revivals swept across China, Manchuria, and Korea. Thousands received Christ as their Savior, and the national churches in those lands enjoyed a level of spiritual life and fruitfulness seldom witnessed since the days of the apostles.

The man whose name is most frequently associated with this movement was Presbyterian missionary Jonathan Goforth. He did not preach divine healing, but in recording the experiences of the revival he noted that in an unexplainable way sick bodies were often healed. One such occasion was the revival movement at Putoupeichen.

> One remarkable thing about these testimonies was the great number who claimed that on that sixth morning when the Spirit's fire had swept so irresistibly through the audience, they had been healed of their bodily ailments. In my addresses I had made no special mention of divine healing. Yet here was the testimony of these people that suddenly, at some crucial moment, that which ailed them passed away. On another occasion, in a neighbouring province, I heard similar testimonies to Divine Healing. In both instances, according to the evidence of the witnesses, the experiences coincided with the moment of most intense conviction.[4]

A. T. Pierson writes of the breakthrough of the gospel among the Eskimos of Greenland. Missionary labor had been fruitless until Hans Egele (1686-1758) called on God for the gift of healing the sick. The Lord heard his cry, and as he prayed sick bodies were made whole. The long-standing indifference of the Eskimos was soon exchanged for spiritual desire and a people was called out for Christ's name from among them.[5]

In 1894, a mighty revival moved through Madagascar. Healing was a very distinct feature of the work of God. A number of medical doctors had opportunity for a first-hand inspection of the healings. Dr. Salomon, an outstanding physician, witnessed the instantaneous healing of a native whose left arm was paralyzed. Tumors, leprosy, and other conditions were healed by prayer. Many were attracted to the gospel by the great demonstrations of the power of Christ in the miracles of healing performed in His name.

The chronicles of worldwide missions record that healing signs have followed the gospel wherever it has been preached from apostolic times until the twentieth century. There is every reason to believe that signs will continue throughout the church age. But care must be taken not to place all healings in the category of "signs."

In both the Old and New Testaments there are two aspects of healing. Distinctly sign miracles of healings are effective in the unconverted as well as in those identified with the community of believers. Healing that may be designated as "the children's bread" is the privilege of believers. Much of the confusion in the modern church could be cleared up by distinguishing these two aspects of healing.

This distinction explains the paradox in Paul's experience. On the island of Miletus he called on the Lord and saw pagan people instantly healed, but when his dear friend and co-worker Trophimus lay sick he had to leave him in that condition. Prayer did not immediately prevail for Trophimus. He eventually recovered but there was a delay.

The healing of the pagans was an example of God's sovereign work of confirming the Word by signs following. Trophimus was a dedicated child of God and his healing was on different ground. Healing for a Christian is governed by conditions related to his spiritual life.

Some scholars have concluded that the above problem in Paul's ministry represented the passing of the dispensational milestone. They say that by the close of Paul's ministry the apostolic healing miracles were on the wane and that he no longer possessed the gift of healing. The New Testament says nothing of the kind. The failure to discriminate between the sign healings and the healing that is the privilege of the believer resulted in this erroneous conclusion.

The healing of a Christian does not occur for the primary purpose of publicly certifying the power of God. A believer's healing may have a public effect, but this is incidental to the spiritual benefit the healing effects in the believer's inner life. The purpose of God is to bring each of us into conformity with the image of His Son, the Lord Jesus Christ. The physical healing of a Christian must be considered in this frame of reference.

Often silently and unnoticed the touch of God brings miraculous restoration to the Christian's body. The believer experiences a divine schooling while suffering physical illness. Healing comes only when the divine process is complete. Significant issues in one's life are uncovered and dealt with. Sickness in the believer can be the chastening of the Lord to bring about spiritual growth. Hence, the difference in the treatment of the subject by the biblical writers. Sign healings and healings of Christians are two quite different manifestations of the healing power of Christ.

Healing signs have continued through the present century. Recent manifestations of "signs following" took place in Nigeria during the "New Life for All" campaign. The evangelistic thrust was preceded by an intense period of preparation during which the Holy Spirit moved on the church with revival blessing. "New Life for All" was an interdenominational program and, therefore, presented a broad spectrum of theology. For the most part the ministry of healing did not make up a regular part of the dogma or practice of the participating churches. However, remarkable incidents of healing did occur quite unsolicited by the churches.

George W. Peters, in his book *Saturation Evangelism*, quotes these reports from an African publication:

> The movement is not devoid of some unique manifestations of the supernatural in the realm of physical divine healing are reported, such as the gradual restoration of sight to a blind woman after prayer for her. A crippled boy of ten years of age was healed. A young girl was instantly cured of consuming fever. God has proven Himself adequate in physically and spiritually meeting the needs of men, and in establishing His presence and loving care.[6]

The August 1968 issue of *Africa Now* relates a miracle of healing reported by a witness team in an African village:

> A team member was accosted by a man whose small son was desperately ill. He thrust the unconscious child at him and said, "If your God is so powerful, have him heal my son." Shaken, the young man accepted the child and offered a fervent prayer. Almost immediately the child began to regain consciousness, and by morning was completely well. Many in that village turned to Christ.

Another area of the world visited by revival in 1965-66 was the island of Timor, East Indonesia, and some neighboring islands. The manifestation of the supernatural was so great as to create worldwide attention at the peak of the revival.

Marion C. Allen of the Christian and Missionary Alliance mission in Indonesia gives a firsthand report:

During the revival in the Protestant Church many outstanding miracles have taken place, attested by reliable witnesses. . . . The ministry of the three or four gospel teams presently active is very good and the Holy Spirit has manifested Himself in the healing of many people. Many have been brought to repentance. Many have burned their fetishes.[7]

The Greek term *semeion,* translated "sign," is defined in Souter's Lexicon as "an outward indication of secret power or truth." In this sense a sign would be a miraculous occurrence. When Christ announced that the church's witness would be attested by supernatural signs, He specifically mentioned the healing of the sick.

The promises of God are, first and foremost, for the believers. That God has freedom to do "signs and wonders" to demonstrate His power and to confirm the gospel must also be granted and believed.

Failure to distinguish creates confusion

Confining healing to "acts of power" and failure to distinguish healing as "the children's bread" can be recognized in dispensational teaching. Identifying all healings as sign miracles has an important bearing on the dispensationalists' position.

Theological presuppositions have blinded many believers to biblical teaching regarding physical healing as a benefit for Christians now. Among modern evangelicals those who embrace the dispensational position are prone to dismiss Christian healing on the ground of dispensational distinction. Obviously, a part of proper Bible study is to discern the "ages" in God's plan. But when a preconceived structure is superimposed on the New Testament or on any other part of the Bible, important truth can be overlooked.

Strong dispensationalists teach that "healing the sick" is strictly a kingdom phenomenon. It occurred in Christ's earthly ministry because He was officially offering the kingdom to the Jews. The kingdom, therefore, is a Jewish matter and was postponed when the Jews crucified the Messiah. The church is a parenthetical interlude until the Jewish kingdom is reinstated and a mass physical healing is anticipated in the kingdom age or the millennial reign of Christ. However, if physical healing occurs only in the kingdom, according to their preconceived structure, no healing should occur at other times.

In fairness, it must be said that dispensationalists for the most part do believe in divine healing and this study should not be interpreted as an effort to refute dispensationalism per se, but rather to examine their position on divine healing.

Louis S. Bauman, a gifted Bible teacher of the dispensational school, writes:

> That God does heal today, not to give mankind signs, but that He may bless by acts of power (in response to the prayer of faith according to His will) the bodies of His saints, which are the temples of the Holy Ghost we dare affirm.[8]

This conception of healing as an *act of power* has important implications. Those who hold that position look upon healings of the present as isolated incidents of sovereign intervention and nothing more.

Dr. Bauman makes an interesting concession with regard to healing in the following statement:

> Surely the promise of healing is there . . . because faith can overcome all barriers, even dispensational barriers if need be (Mark 7:24-30 with Matt. 8:10).[9]

This is a classic example of overemphasis on dispensational distinctions. It seems rather strange that a child of

God should have to carry on a battle of faith to cross a dispensational line in order to have the help of God for the healing of his body.

In the Scriptures from Genesis to Revelation it can be seen that physical healing by divine intervention has occurred in every age. Healing knows no dispensational boundaries.

The following quotation is another example of the stance taken by dispensational theologians with regard to relationship between miracles and the kingdom:

> (The miracles of Christ) are so related to the kingdom that they cannot be separated from it without mutual deface-ment. Thus it is represented by Jesus Himself (Matt. 12:28), "But if I cast out devils by the Spirit of God, then the king-dom of God is come unto (or as some, upon) you." Here we have,
>
> 1. The relationship existing between the kingdom and miracles; that without the latter the former cannot be revealed.
> 2. That miracles are a manifestation of possessed power, which Jesus will exert when He establishes this kingdom.
>
> Every miracle which the Lord performed, then, may be understood to be not only a demonstration of the theocratic power of the Messiah, but also that which depicts the conditions which will exist in the theocratic kingdom when it is established.[10]

Both the above typical examples of the dispensational viewpoint assume that Jesus and His disciples healed the sick for the sole reason of certifying the kingdom message. Such an interpretation rules out the very nature of Christ's response to human need—the personal aspects of the gospel records of healing.

Faith was a frequent necessity for a healing touch. Christ described for some who came to Him for healing conditions to be met peculiar to their own case. These facts gleaned from gospel accounts would indicate that Jesus dealt with these cases on the basis of a regard for their personal problems. Christ was interested in the sick as persons. His healing ministry cannot be limited to the certification of the kingdom of God. In fact, the "sign aspect" seems secondary to Christ's obvious compassion for suffering people.

The healing ministry of the eternal Christ embraces all the healings of the Bible. It seems appropriate that the hand of Jehovah-*rapha* which healed Abimelech's household, Miriam, King Hezekiah, and Naaman the Syrian should also heal the sick when He walked on earth incarnate in human flesh. It may be expected that Christ will also heal the sick when He comes again as King of kings to reign on earth.

The need for a proper perspective

When divine healing is not recognized as "the children's bread" and is confused with "signs and wonders," the result is a truncated gospel—a gospel that is restricted to a spiritualism that fails to minister to the wholeness of man's need and inhibits the redemptive resources that ought to be generated as a Christian life style. Healing is part of the "gospel loaf" and if accepted as such, will add a dimension that was intended for its message and mission.

Dr. Simpson caught the significance of healing as "the children's bread" when he wrote:

> When Christ heals, He does not do it through a logical necessity that He should keep His promise, but He does it with His whole heart and soul. He is sorry for your pain. He is so glad to help you. Then this touch of Christ implies also a direct contact between the Lord and the sufferer. Healing is not mere answer to prayer. It is not a package delivered

from heaven through a messenger; but it is a meeting between you and the Lord. It is a personal contact with the
living Christ.[11]

When God's redemptive purpose is seen as the ground
on which faith may be exercised, the fuller relationships
and privileges of the believer become significant. Instead
of physical healing being narrowly utilitarian and only
accidentally related to God's plan and program of redemption, it becomes deeply personal.

Failure to distinguish between divine healing as "the
children's bread" and "signs and wonders" will cause
a lack of discernment when healings do take place in mixed
situations, where unregenerate people are healed. Healing
incidents too often are looked upon as a strange phenomenon
easily associated with magic and superstition and not as
God's own divine provisions. Even God's people are prone
to look to human healers rather than to the Lord. Cultic
tendencies are difficult to check when charismatic enthusi-
asts, who are largely experience-oriented in their theology,
gain recognition. Whenever a vacuum of doctrinal truth
is allowed to develop unchecked, heresy is sure to follow.

Modern interest in the occult reflects man's search for
a source of healing that is essentially spiritual; this can
open the human personality to dangerous forces. Christian
healing relates to the whole body of biblical truth and has
a theology; the doctrine of healing for man's physical
needs is part of the theology of redemption that is both
individual and cosmic.

The Christian is called to be a changed person and to
live by the standards of Christ's kingdom in a culture that
needs a new direction and a demonstration of the power of
the gospel. By this standard life in its entirety is to be
wholesomely Christian and, as such, does not need to

hide in an aura of mysticism. Christ is Creator-Redeemer, the Meaning-giver and Judge of life.

[1] W. C. Stevens, *Revelation, the Crown Jewel of Prophecy,* 1:437.

[2] John L. Nevius, *Demon Possession,* p. 362.

[3] Marie Monsen, *The Awakening: Revival in China, a Work of the Holy Spirit,* p. 84.

[4] Jonathan Goforth, *By My Spirit,* p. 106.

[5] Arthur T. Pierson, *The New Acts of the Apostles,* p. 84.

[6] George W. Peters, *Saturation Evangelism,* p. 118.

[7] Marion C. Allen, "What Happened in the Timor Revival?" *The Pioneer,* April 1970, pp. 20-21.

[8] Louis S. Bauman, *The Faith Once for All Delivered unto the Saints,* p. 84.

[9] *Ibid.,* p. 85.

[10] J. Dwight Pentecost, *Things to Come: A Study in Biblical Eschatology,* pp. 451-52.

[11] A. B. Simpson, "Christ's First Message About Healing," *Alliance Weekly,* August 31, 1929, p. 567.

3

Healing and
the Atonement

THE PRIVILEGE OF PHYSICAL healing is considered
by some in the church as an act of God's power sovereignly
given. To others healing is an inheritance vouchsafed to
the believer on the ground of Christ's atoning death. Most
of the controversy regarding the doctrine of divine healing
stems from the tension between these two points of view.

The claim for healing in the atonement rests on two
principal passages of Scripture: Isaiah 53:4-5 and Matthew
8:17.

> *Surely our griefs (sickness,* margin) *He Himself bore,*
> *And our sorrows (pain,* margin) *He carried;*
> *Yet we ourselves esteemed Him stricken,*
> *Smitten of God, and afflicted.*
> *But He was pierced through for our transgressions,*
> *He was crushed for our iniquities;*
> *The chastening for our well-being fell upon Him,*
> *And by His scourging we are healed* (Isa. 53:4-5).

> *And when evening had come, they brought to Him*
> *many who were demon-possessed; and He cast out the*
> *spirits with a word, and healed all who were ill; in*
> *order that what was spoken through Isaiah the prophet*
> *might be fulfilled, saying, "He Himself took our*
> *infirmities, and carried away our diseases"* (Matt.
> 8:16-17).

A. B. Simpson says of these passages:

This is the great evangelical vision, the gospel in the Old
Testament, the very mirror of the coming Redeemer. And
here in the front of it, prefaced by a great Amen—the only
"surely" in the chapter—is the promise of healing; the very
strongest possible statement of complete redemption from
pain and sickness by His life and death, and the very words
which the Evangelist afterwards quotes, under inspired
guidance of the Holy Ghost (Matt. 8:17) as the explanation
of His universal works of healing.[1]

R. Kelso Carter, one of Dr. Simpson's early co-workers,
said the following as to the manner in which healing is in
the atonement:

The clear meaning is, that Jesus did take upon Himself our
diseases and our mental trouble, in precisely the same way
that He "bore our sins in His own body on the tree."[2]

Simpson and Carter were not alone in their position on
healing in the atonement. An impressive list of writers
made similar statements expressing the belief that as Christ
took our sins upon Himself He also took our sicknesses.
Many scholars now object to this position. They admit
that in some way healing is in the atonement but not in the
same manner as sin.

Controversy over this issue raged in the day of Simpson.
The burning question was, How is healing in the atonement? All kinds of theories were proposed to explain Mat-

thew 8:17. The opponents of healing maintained that Jesus did not bear sickness as He bore sin. They proposed that Christ bore sickness in some other way than the cross. Carter is insisting that the manner in which Christ bore our sicknesses was by means of His vicarious death on the cross.

A. J. Gordon, an outstanding Baptist minister of the nineteenth century and the founder of Gordon College, Boston, saw the atonement as a foundation for faith in healing.

> In the atonement of Christ there seems to be a foundation laid for faith in bodily healing, seems—we say, for the passage to which we refer is so profound and unsearchable in its meaning that one would be very careful not to speak dogmatically in regard to it. But it is at least a deep and suggestive truth that we have Christ set before us as the sickness bearer as well as the sin bearer of His people. In the Gospel it is written, "And he cast out devils and healed all that were sick, that it might be fulfilled which was spoken by Esaias the prophet saying, Himself took our infirmities and bore our sicknesses." Something more than sympathetic fellowship with our suffering is evidently referred to here. The yoke of his cross by which he lifted our iniquities took hold also of our diseases; so that it is in some sense true that as God "made him to be sin for us who knew no sin," so he made him to be sick for us who knew no sickness. He who entered into mysterious sympathy with our pain which is the fruit of sin, also put himself underneath our pain which is the penalty of sin. In other words the passage seems to teach that Christ endured vicariously our diseases as well as our iniquities.[3]

This statement is a classic presentation of healing in the atonement, and some attempts have been made to prove a note of hesitancy in Dr. Gordon's stand. The passage quoted deals with ultimate redemptive consequences for man.

> We hold that in its ultimate consequences the atonement
> affects the body, as well as the soul of man. Sanctification
> is the consummation of Christ's redemptive work for the
> soul, and the resurrection is the consummation of His re-
> demptive work for the body.[4]

Rowland Bingham interprets this quotation as an effort
to modify the claims of his contemporaries regarding the
extent of the atonement as covering physical disease. When
read in its context, however, this was an obvious effort
to put the teaching of healing in the atonement into some
kind of theological perspective.

Gordon understood that the benefit of healing, like
other redemptive benefits, could be claimed and enjoyed
to the extent a redeemed man's present state will permit.
The benefit of healing in the atonement does not demand
that all who exercise faith must have perfect health any
more than the benefit of salvation in the atonement demands
that all who believe must manifest complete sinlessness.

The opponents of Gordon and Simpson admit that
healing must in some way be in the atonement. Bingham
says:

> To that statement no orthodox theologian will take excep-
> tion; nor with the further argument that there are present
> possible benefits that flow from the atonement made for
> our sins which affect in some measure the health and healing
> of the body.[5]

In the fall of 1917 Benjamin Warfield delivered the
Thomas Smith Lectures at Columbia Theological Seminary. His subject was "Counterfeit Miracles." He deals
with the healing movement from a typical reformed position regarding miracles. Concerned with the teaching that
healing was in the atonement, Warfield cites both Gordon
and Otto Stockmayer as holding an untenable position
regarding Isaiah 53 and Matthew 8:17. He attacks their

position on the ground that it violates the reformed view of the atonement. But Warfield does make the following concession regarding the relationship of healing to the atonement:

> It will doubtless be more profitable, however, to seek to lay our finger on the source of error in the statement of the doctrine, and to correct it, than to track out all its confusions. This error does not lie in the supposition that redemption is for the body as well as the soul and that the saved man shall be renewed in the one as well as the other. This is true. Nor does it lie in the supposition that provision is made in the atonement for the relief of men from disease and suffering, which are the fruits of sin. This too is true. It lies in confusing redemption itself which is objective and takes place outside of us, with its subjective effects, which take place in us; and in failing to recognize that these subjective effects of redemption are wrought in gradually and in a definite order.[6]

Warfield is here admitting that the Scriptures do teach redemption for the body and that the atonement does include the relief of man's disease and suffering. In this same discourse he concedes that there is an intermediate healing. Warfield saw healing as a by-product of the gospel's effect upon man. He seems to overlook the obvious conclusion of his own argument. If the atonement is admitted to be the procuring cause of Christ's healing ministry to the bodies of redeemed men and if there is an intermediate healing of men's bodies while in their present state, then that healing must be the direct, not the indirect, benefit of the atonement.

Paul Jewett, of Fuller Theological Seminary, treats healing in the atonement in much the same way as Warfield. Jewett says:

> Speaking of the perfection of the Atonement, a word should be said about divine healing. Healing is commonly asso-

ciated with faith, but ultimately it has to do with the Atonement. "Faith healing" presupposes that in the Atonement
our Lord contemplated the body as well as the soul. So those
who stress healing of the body, if they spell out their doctrine
beyond a general faith in God, would say that the faith
which heals is a faith in the Savior who Himself took our
infirmities and bore our diseases (Matt. 8:17). Not to trust
Christ for deliverance from the afflictions of the body, as
well as the sins of the soul, is to impugn the perfection of
His atoning work. Evangelicals have never doubted the efficacy of the Atonement for the whole man, affirming the
resurrection of the body, so that Christ's death became the
"death of deaths" for all who die in Him. But the obvious
fact that all men die in a physical way, even those who proclaim faith healing, has led the church as a whole to conclude that the redemptive benefits of the Atonement, as far
as the body is concerned, must wait the *eschaton,* when
there shall be no more curse, neither sorrow nor crying nor
any such thing (Rev. 2:4).[7]

In concluding that the church as a whole has adopted
the view that the redemptive benefits to the body must
await the *eschaton,* Jewett apparently elects to overlook
the vast body of literature from the ancient church, the
medieval church, and the modern church proclaiming
physical healing as a present possibility. Literally hundreds
of pages of prayers, liturgies, homilies, historical records,
and theological treatments are ample testimony that a large
part of the church concluded the availability of healing
through faith and prayer.

Jewett rejects physical healing as an intermediate benefit
of the atonement on the ground that all men die physically.
It is difficult to understand how the reality of physical
death can nullify healing for the believer. The biblical
doctrine of healing does not claim to conquer death. Death
is defeated by the resurrection—the ultimate result of the
atonement. All of the people Christ healed had to die.
Certainly no serious scholar would discredit His miracles

of healing on the ground that the recipients of that blessing ultimately died.

Jewett, like Warfield, fails to see the obvious conclusion of his own argument. The establishment of the efficacy of the atonement for the whole man opens the door to its immediate effect upon the body as well as its ultimate effect.

The aggregate of all the Epistles have to say about physical healing provides ample evidence that the believer may eat the children's bread now. The healing of the body is the firstfruits of the coming resurrection.

Reuben A. Torrey, while president of Moody Bible Institute, wrote on the subject of healing in the atonement. Dr. Torrey had an excellent academic background and a worldwide reputation as an evangelist. He was the successor to D. L. Moody. Torrey believed Matthew 8:17 to teach healing in the atonement, but he cautions believers as to their conclusion drawn from that fact. Torrey wrote:

> It is often said that this verse teaches that the atoning death of Jesus Christ avails for our sicknesses as well as for our sins; or in other words, that physical healing is in the atonement. I think this is a fair inference from these verses taken in their context.
>
> But while we do not get the full benefits for the body secured for us by the atoning death of Jesus Christ in the life that now is but when Jesus comes again, nevertheless, just as one gets the first fruits of his spiritual salvation in the life that now is, so we get the first fruits of our physical salvation in the life that now is. We do get in many, many, many cases of physical healing through the atoning death of Jesus Christ even in the life that now is.[8]

R. L. Stanton, a prominent Presbyterian minister who at one time served as moderator of the Presbyterian Church in the U.S.A., while on a trip to England discovered the truth of divine healing. He frequented the Bethshan Con-

ferences conducted by W. E. Boardman. It became Stanton's firm conviction that healing was in the atonement.
Commenting on Matthew 8:17 he says:

> St. Matthew here applies these words of the Prophet, respect-
> ing the atoning work of the Messiah, as having their fulfill-
> ment in Christ's healing of the sick. If, therefore, plain
> language has any force, it were impossible to state more
> explicitly than the inspired evangelist does, that the healing
> of the sick was one of the blessings which Christ's atone-
> ment was designed for; that this was Isaiah's meaning in the
> passage referred to, and that this was a part of the mission
> which Christ publicly inaugurated for the ministry of the
> New Dispensation.[9]

The key to the meaning of Isaiah 53:4 is to be found in
Matthew 8:17. Matthew quotes the Septuagint translation
of Isaiah 53:4 with one alteration. He substitutes *elaben*
for *phero*. This change in wording has been interpreted as
a change in the meaning of the passage. Bingham, Frost,
and Beiderwulf all assume that Matthew's use of a different
verb means that the atonement is not in view. They seek
to prove that Jesus bore sickness in some manner other
than His cross.

Bingham maintains that Christ bore human sickness in
His life and not in His death. By His concern and sympathy
Christ bore the sufferings of sick people. Bingham does
not bother to explain what he means by Jesus bearing sick-
ness in His life. His position implies that Christ lived an
atoning life. This is a heresy he vigorously condemned.
Bingham believed that Christ bore man's sicknesses in
Capernaum, not at Calvary.

Henry Frost's explanation of the quotation from Isaiah
53 found in Matthew 8:17 is typical of the effort of some
theologians to dodge the issue of atonement in this passage.

> It appears, therefore, that Isa. 53:4,5 was written with a
> double prophetic outlook; first to an atonement for sin, of

which Peter speaks (I Peter 2:24); and second, to the healing of disease, before and apart from the atonement, of which Matthew speaks (Matt. 8:17) this last, undoubtedly, as an evidence and proof of Christ's messianic claims. This double significance, if a rightful interpretation is to be reached, must be kept in view, and the two must be held separate and must not be confused. In other words, Matt. 8:17 does not refer to the atoning work of Christ, and universal healing cannot be founded upon it. It refers to a temporary content connected with the earthly ministry of our Lord, which being "fulfilled" was not to be renewed.[10]

The Greek verb *elaben* that Matthew employs in 8:17 is used several times in the Septuagint to translate the Hebrew verb *nasa*. In a number of passages in Leviticus (e.g., 16:22) the word carries the sense of bearing sin, especially to bear the punishment occasioned by sin. It is clearly used to express expiation.

> *And the goat shall bear on itself all their iniquities to a solitary land; and he shall release the goat in the wilderness* (Lev. 16:22).

The setting for this passage is the Day of Atonement. No levitical ritual more clearly pictures the vicarious atonement of Christ than the dual offerings for atonement described in Leviticus 16. The scapegoat vicariously bore away Israel's sins. The scapegoat portrays the removal of sin as the effect of atonement. The import of *elaben* is distinctly expiation.

To make Matthew 8:17 something other than atonement is to weaken this doctrine. This very issue was the eye of the theological storm during the last half of the nineteenth century. Bushnell appealed to the Matthew passage to establish his governmental theory of the atonement. He saw Christ bearing our sicknesses in His life rather than in His death. On this ground he reasoned that the atonement was God's sympathy rather than satisfaction as the Scriptures teach.

It seems incredible that all the evangelical scholars who attacked the teaching of healing in the atonement followed Bushnell's error in their interpretation of Matthew 8:17 without realizing the implications of Bushnell's teaching.

A. A. Hodge, late professor of Systematic Theology at Princeton from 1877 to 1886, pointed out the fallacy of making the "bearing" of Matthew 8:17 anything less than atonement.

> Bushnell says that Matthew's reference (Matt. VIII:17) to Isaiah LIII:4 "is the one scripture citation that gives beyond question the exact *usu loquendi* of all the vicarious and sacrificial language of the New Testament." The passage in Isaiah is as follows: "Surely he hath borne (Hebrew *nasa*; Septuagint *phero*) our griefs, and carried (Hebrew *sabal*) our sorrows." The reference in Matthew is: "And he cast out the spirits with his word, and healed all that were sick; that it might be fulfilled which was spoken by Esaias the prophet, saying, himself took (*elaben*) our infirmities and bore our sicknesses." From this datum Bushnell draws two amazing conclusions: (1) That the exact *usus loquendi* of all vicarious and sacrificial language in the New Testament is to be derived from this single passage. (2) That the only sense in which Christ bore either our sins, our sorrows, or our diseases was that he took them on his feelings—had his heart burdened with the sense of them.
>
> To the first assumption we answer that the *usus loguendi* of the words can be determined only by a careful analysis and comparison of all passages in which they severally occur in the original Hebrew, in the Septuagint, and in the New Testament itself.
>
> To the second assumption, we answer that it is a notorious fact, admitted by all scholars, that the New Testament writers quote the Old Testament freely, accommodating the sense to a present purpose. Isaiah affirms that Christ bore our sorrows, that is, bore them on himself in order to remove them. Isaiah uses the technical words *nasa* and *sabal*; the Septuagint translates *phero*, but Matthew substitutes *elaben*.

There is no contradiction, only Isaiah emphasized the *carried*, and Matthew emphasized the *removed*. The first pointed out the means, the other the result effected. The fact is he endured visible sorrows, which made men believe that he was under divine chastisement; hence it is said, "We thought Him stricken, smitten of God, and afflicted . . . but he was wounded for our transgressions, the punishment of our peace was upon him."[11]

Franz Delitzsch, Hebrew professor at the University of Leipzig, Germany, wrote on the necessity of vicarious atonement in Matthew 8:17, making this observation:

Matthew's Gospel (in chap. VIII. 17) here corrects the LXX by translating thus: *autos tas astheneias hemon elaben kai tas nosous ebastasen*; and the relief which Jesus afforded to all kinds of bodily ailments is regarded as a fulfillment of these words. . . . Matthew appropriately renders *nasa* by *elaben* and *nabal* by *ebastasen*; for, while *nabal* signifies the toilsome bearing of a burden that has been taken up, *nasa* combines in itself the idea presented by *tollere* and *ferre.* Construed with the accusative of the sin, it means to take on one's self the guilt of sin as one's own, and to bear it, i.e. to recognize and feel it as such, as in Lev. V. 1,17; more frequently it means to bear the punishment incurred through sin, i.e. to come to make atonement for it, as in Lev. XVII. 16, XX. 19f, XXIV. 15, and wherever the bearer himself is not the guilty one, to bear the sin as a mediator, in order to atone for it, Lev. X. 17. . . . In the LXX this *nasa* is rendered, both in the Penteteuch and in Ezekiel, by *labein harmartian*, once by *anapherein*; this *labein* and *anapherein* are meant to be understood as referring to expiatory bearing, and not merely, as has been affirmed, in opposition to vicarious satisfaction, in the sense of taking away, is abundantly shown in Ezekiel IV. 4-8 where the *seh aow* is represented by the prophet in symbolical action. Even here, where it is not the sins, but "our sicknesses"—and "our pains" that form the object, the meaning is that the Servant of God took upon himself the sufferings which we had to bear, and deserved to bear, and endured them in his own person, in order to deliver us from them.[12]

A third scholar who dealt with this mediatorial aspect of Matthew 8:17 was Joseph A. Alexander, distinguished Hebrew and Oriental scholar of Princeton Theological Seminary. Alexander's work on Isaiah first appeared in print in 1847 and has remained a classic on the writing of the prophet. He says of Isaiah 53:

> The application of these words by Matthew (viii:17) to the removal of bodily diseases cannot involve a denial of the doctrine of vicarious atonement, which is clearly recognized in Matt. xx 28, nor is it an exposition of the passage quoted in its full sense, but as Calvin well explains it, an intimation that the prediction had begun to be fulfilled, because already its effects were visible, the Scripture always representing sorrow as the fruit of sin.[13]

Melancthon Jacobus, a professor of biblical literature at Western Theological Seminary in Allegany City, Pennsylvania, prepared for the American Sunday School Union a commentary on Matthew. In his treatment of 8:17 he explains why healing is in the atonement.

> Matthew, writing for Jews, aims to connect Christ's doings with their own inspired prophecies, and so to identify Him to them as their Messiah. "He that put away sin by the sacrifice of Himself," and "bore our sins in His own body on the tree," undertook to put away all the fruits of sin. This is the connection of His healing with His atonement.[14]

Jacobus isolates the central truth of this passage. Physical healing is related to vicarious atonement because sickness in man is the direct result of his fallen state. Christ dealt with sickness by dealing with sin. This answers the question, How is healing in the atonement? The perfect atonement of Jesus Christ dealt so completely with sin as to effect the putting away of the fruits of sin.

The Isaiah 53 passage plus the quotation from this chapter by Matthew and its inspired interpretation constitute a forthright biblical statement that healing is in the atonement.

The doctrine of healing in the atonement says not that universal healing is therefore available, but rather that physical healing is available to believers on the ground of the blood atonement. The blood of Christ is the procuring cause of healing as a benefit to believers.

The Scriptures do make the blood atonement the procuring cause of healing. But candor must be used in interpreting the fact. Dr. Simpson and his colleagues were aware of the abuses associated with this teaching. J. H. Oerter raised the question of the practical implications of physical healing being in the atonement.

> If then, Christ has thus atoned for the physical and mental consequences of sin not less than for sin itself the question arises, which rights and privileges is faith permitted to derive from that fact?[15]

Oerter cautions his readers regarding the limitations Scripture imposes on the claims of faith. He did not teach that because healing was in the atonement healing should immediately occur in every instance. This kind of exaggeration came when fringe groups became enamored with the doctrine of healing and began to teach it without regard to its theological moorings.

Fredrick W. Farr, early professor of theology at the Missionary Training Institute, treated the matter of healing in the atonement with great wisdom.

> Scripture teaches that the satisfaction of Christ in making atonement covers the body as well as the soul of man. We must all admit an insoluble mystery in the atonement. Faith must accept a conclusion on the authority of God's Word that reason cannot reach alone. We do not know how Jesus could bear our sins in such wise as He did being sinless, but we believe the word. (I Peter 2:24; II Cor. 5:21), and, on test-

ing its reality, we receive a definite and conscious experience of pardoned sin. We do not know how Jesus could bear our sicknesses, but the two passages quoted above referring to sin are exactly paralleled by Isaiah 53:4,10. "Surely our sicknesses he hath borne . . . He hath made him sick" (Young's translation). These words refer properly to bodily diseases and are so interpreted by an inspired commentator in Matt. 8:16, 17. We may believe this testimony of God's Word concerning sickness as we do that touching sin, without understanding it, and on testing its reality, we receive definite and conscious experience of physical healing. This is all that is commonly implied by the saying that we see divine healing in the atonement.[16]

The Scriptures state that healing is in the atonement but they do not disclose how healing is in the atonement. Both the friends and the critics of this teaching have sometimes misread the implication of healing in the atonement. Physical healing is not necessarily available to God's people because the body is included in the atonement. J. Hudson Ballard, early teacher at Nyack, shares remarkable insight on this subject in his book *Spirit, Soul and Body.*

It is not enough to learn that a certain blessing is provided by the atonement; if we would enjoy that blessing in this life, we must also ascertain whether that particular portion of the atonement privilege is accessible in this life. All that shall ever come to us from God, both in this life and in the life to come, is through the atonement.

It is not enough therefore to prove that a blessing is in the atonement to assure us that this particular blessing may not be included in the large proportion of atonement privileges which are to be experienced only in the life to come. Absolute sinlessness, for instance, is ours through the atonement, but it is to be ours in fullness only in the future life. Again, a condition of body not subject to weariness is purchased by the atonement, but will not be enjoyed in this life. Further, the resurrection body complete is in the atonement for us, but we are not to experience it until the beginning of the next dispensation.

How may it be now concerning the redemption of the mind? And it might be added parenthetically, How may it be concerning the healing of the body? A great many who believe in divine healing think that the question is settled entirely if they can prove that healing is in the atonement, but this by itself in no wise makes it certain that healing is a present day possibility. It may be one of those atonement blessings which belong to the next life. Fortunately we have abundant evidence in the Scriptures that healing is for us in this very dispensation. The same is true of redemption for the mind.[17]

Ballard rightly concludes that while the atonement is the proper procuring cause of physical healing as a redemptive benefit to believers, the availability of healing now is based on propositional statements in the Scriptures. This is consistent with all other redemptive blessings. No one would argue the fact that the translation of the believer is in the atonement, but that fact is not sufficient to claim that blessing at any time. Clear scriptural statements indicate that translation is an ultimate redemptive blessing to be enjoyed at Christ's coming. Following this hermeneutical principle, physical healing as an immediate privilege of the believer can be established. The promises and instructions as to how healing may be attained provide abundant proof that physical healing is available today for God's people.

[1] A. B. Simpson, *The Gospel of Healing*, pp. 15-16.

[2] R. Kelso Carter, *The Atonement for Sin and Sickness*, p. 32.

[3] A. J. Gordon, *The Ministry of Healing*, pp. 16-17.

[4] *Ibid.*, p. 18.

[5] R. V. Bingham, *The Bible and The Body*, p. 18.

[6] Benjamin Warfield, *Miracles, Yesterday and Today*, p. 176.

[7]*The Zondervan Pictorial Encyclopedia of the Bible,* s.v. "Atonement," by P. Jewett.

[8]Reuben A. Torrey, *Divine Healing*, pp. 28-29.

[9]R. L. Stanton, *Gospel Parallelisms, Healing for Body and Soul,* p. 17.

[10]Henry W. Frost, *Miraculous Healing,* p. 59.

[11]Archibald A. Hodges, *The Atonement,* pp. 177-78.

[12]Franz Delitzsch, *Biblical Commentary on the Prophecies of Isaiah*, 2:291-92.

[13]Joseph A. Alexander, *Commentary on the Prophecies of Isaiah*, p. 294.

[14]Melancthon W. Jacobus, *Notes on the Gospels,* p. 96.

[15]J. H. Oerter, *Divine Healing in the Light of Scripture,* p. 68.

[16]Fredrick W. Farr, *A Manual of Christian Doctrine,* pp. 114-15.

[17]J. Hudson Ballard, *Spirit, Soul and Body,* pp. 157-58.

4

Healing in Early
Biblical History

THE CHURCH MUST DRAW her doctrine from the
wellsprings of Scripture. While the long history of this
doctrine, which embraces every age of the church, is impressive, the proof of historical theology is not enough.

What does the Bible say about physical healing? The
revelation of the Old Testament lays the foundation for
the doctrine of physical healing.

In the shadow of Eden

The book of Genesis has been called the "seed plot" of
the Scriptures. Many concepts of spiritual truth that are
developed during the unfolding of divine revelation are
introduced in this first book of the Bible. At least six
passages touch upon the doctrine of healing.

The first Bible reference to man's physical health,
Genesis 4:26, goes unnoticed by the casual reader:

> *And to Seth, to him also a son was born; and he called his name Enosh.*

The name *Enos* or *Enosh* in the Hebrew is rarely used in the singular and becomes a poetic expression signifying "mortal" or "frail."[1] As an appellative it is a generic word for "man" and is applied to the whole human race. Two other words in the Hebrew are used for *man: adam* and *ish* (Gen. 2:7, 23).

With Enos began a new religious development—"Then men began to call upon the name of the Lord" (Gen. 4:26) —which suggests a contrast to former practice, perhaps the beginning of formal divine worship. In Seth, who represents the line of Abel who was murdered by Cain, is propagated this patriarch who sets an example of seeking the living God.

Man is subject to death; he is mortal and represents a "living death" unless there is a deliverer who can be called upon. In early Hebrew thought, both life and death had a strong singular meaning because the resurrection and immortality in Christ had not unveiled the relationships of soul and body. Men began to call on the name of the Lord because a new dimensional consciousness of an eternal world was being awakened as evil began to rise to an insolent defiance and threat to human life (Gen. 4:23 ff.). Chapter four is followed by chapter five with its repetitive ringing words *and he died,* but until Enos death had been rare.

Modern expressions tend to set the spiritual dimension of man as a specific department alongside other departments, his "religious interests" alongside other interests, but this is not the biblical view. All of human life is to be oriented to the Absolute. The early Hebrews knew nothing about departmentalizing man.

Enos was seeking the unifying principle to his existence and fought the fragmentizing effect sin was producing by calling on his Creator for physical and spiritual deliverance. The memory of Eden and God's perfect creation was now burdened with a consciousness of sin's destructiveness; and though the longevity of man had not yet been affected as it was immediately after the flood, man began to call on God for deliverance.

The promise of "the seed of the woman"

All the recorded healings in the Genesis period were related to the physical problem of barrenness. God had declared to Satan that the "seed of the woman" would bruise his head (Gen. 3:15), and the godly line destined to bring Christ into the world was afflicted with Satan's opposition to the fulfillment of that prediction.

Abraham and Sarah

After Abraham obeyed in leaving Haran and had come to the plains of Moreh, the Lord appeared to him and promised that his seed would inherit the land of Canaan (Gen. 12:7). But Abraham's wife, Sarah, was barren. After a long time the Lord promised to Abraham not only the inheritance, but a son to be born from his "own body" (Gen. 15:4). But the struggle continued between Abraham and the promise God had made; more time elapsed until Sarah was far past the age for bearing children.

That Sarah would be healed was announced a full year in advance. Three angelic strangers visited Abraham's tent on the plains of Mamre to tell him of this miracle (Gen. 18). One of the three was the Angel of the Lord and is identified as the Lord Himself, believed by many Bible scholars to be the form of the preexistent Christ—the same Christ who would some day walk in Canaan's land and quicken sick bodies by His touch. He came personally to announce to Abraham that He would give him a son by performing a miracle of healing upon Sarah. The announcement made by the Heavenly Visitor seemed so incredible that Sarah laughed, but when Jehovah visited her according to His promise she was able to conceive.

Sarah's subsequent history is remarkable, her youthful beauty apparently becoming a problem to Abraham in the year that followed. He became alarmed at the possibility that he might be destroyed and one of the powerful Canaanite rulers would then take Sarah as his wife. This drove him to lying about Sarah, saying that she was his sister.

The twentieth chapter of Genesis relates the incomplete obedience of Abraham and Sarah while residing in the land of Gerar, occupied by the chieftain Abimelech who feared God and knew His ways. To form an alliance with the wealthy nomad Abraham, Abimelech took Sarah into his sheikdom. Then God appeared to him in a dream and said, "Behold, you are a dead man because of the woman whom you have taken, for she is married" (Gen. 20:3).

Abraham was summarily rebuked and Sarah was restored to her husband, and the curse of barrenness that had come upon Abimelech's wife and maidservants and the impotence that had come upon Abimelech was healed at a specific occurrence:

> *And Abraham prayed to God; and God healed Abimelech and his wife and his maids, so that they bore children. For the Lord had closed fast all the wombs of the household of Abimelech because of Sarah, Abraham's wife* (Gen. 20:17-18).

The Scripture is very exact in the use of the word *heal.*

The physical disability involved is treated as an infirmity and the recovery that followed is described as a "healing," using the Hebrew verb *rapha.*

Isaac and Rebekah

Isaac's experience was similar to that of his father, Abraham. His wife, Rebekah, also was unable to conceive.

And Isaac prayed to the Lord on behalf of his wife, because she was barren; and the Lord answered him and Rebekah his wife conceived (Gen. 25:21).

The simplicity of the account reveals the privilege of God's children to claim by prayer what is inherent in the covenant relationship. The natural and supernatural are so blended as to belong to man's wholeness and sanctified destiny. Martin Luther makes the observation that until this point in Scripture the only prayers recorded of the patriarchs had to do with deliverance for a physical need.[2]

Jacob and Rachel

Jacob's experience follows in the train of Abraham and Isaac.

So Jacob went in to Rachel also, and indeed he loved Rachel more than Leah, and he served with Laban for another seven years.

Now the Lord saw that Leah was unloved, and He opened her womb, but Rachel was barren (Gen. 29: 30-31).

Later, Rachel prayed to God.

> Then God remembered Rachel, and God gave heed to
> her and opened her womb. So she conceived and bore
> a son and said, "God has taken away my reproach"
> (Gen. 30:22-23).

Rachel's ability to conceive and give birth to a son was
recognized as an answer to her prayer though it apparently
took place in God's providence without the signature of a
predictable event. Rachel's son Joseph stands in a unique
relationship to God's purpose and plan.

Healing need not be a sign miracle; it is in the province
of God's children to bring their physical infirmity to God.
God is glorified and His people are blessed when they
recognize answers to prayer though other men do not
recognize the miracle. There is no reason to believe that
Rachel's answer to prayer was any less a miracle than that
of Sarah or of Rebekah when seen from God's vantage
point.

Shalom

The scriptural reflection on health is curiously implied in
the use of the word *shalom*. In Genesis 29, Jacob arrives
at his mother's home community and inquires of his Uncle
Laban. When asking of his uncle's state of health, Jacob
employs the Hebrew salutatory word *shalom* (v. 6). H. C.
Leupold describes the meaning of this word as "a state
of well being in which nothing essential is lacking."[3]

> Franz Delitzsch comments on this passage and the word
> *shalom:* How profound a fact it is, that the Old Testament
> language has the same word for health or soundness, . . . and
> peace . . . When in the relations and mutual relations of the
> bodily, and physical, and spiritual powers, peace prevails,
> the man is sound, . . . a condition which, since sin has gained
> possession of humanity, is never predictable in an absolute,

but merely in a relative manner. Sickness is dissolution of this relative harmony.[4]

Recently Douglas J. Harris, professor of religion at William Jewel College, wrote a thesis at Edinburgh on the biblical concept of peace. Dr. Harris explains the Hebrew idea of health as contained in the word *shalom.*

> It is easy to see how the root meaning of wholeness would relate to health and well-being. . . . The common greeting or salutation *shalom* (I Sam. 10:4; I Chron. 18:10) is wishing for health, the well-being, the *shalom* of the one greeted. . . . Without using the word 'psychosomatic,' the Hebrew realized that spiritual, mental and emotional strains were related to one's health and well-being.[5]

This concept of health fits the biblical revelation regarding the nature of man. God made man spirit, soul, and body. Health for man is a state of harmony between the parts which make him a whole person.

The provisional power of God in Exodus

The book of Exodus expands the Genesis contemplation on the subject of healing. Destitute of all natural help, God's people are to discover the ample provisions and resources that are to be found in their covenant relationship to the Lord.

Moses' leprous hand

The power of working miracles as presented in Exodus 4:1-9 reveals that signs and wonders are given for their evidential value to accredit divinely sent messengers and to confirm God's providential hand at crucial times. The gift of miracles was used for Moses to persuade the Israelites in bondage and to confront Pharaoh that he had been sent as a messenger from God. It was used to confirm Jesus as the Messiah (Acts 2:22; 10:38) and to confirm the apostles as messengers of the gospel (Acts 2:43; 5:12; 14:3). God used healing as a sign miracle

> *"that they may believe that the Lord, the God of their fathers, the God of Abraham, the God of Isaac, and the God of Jacob, has appeared to you"* (Exod. 4:5).

The reluctance of Moses to accept the task of leadership was dealt with by certain sign miracles. God used them to instruct Moses of God's intent to directly intervene for the deliverance of Israel. One such sign was the healing of Moses' hand of leprosy. Moses was instructed to place his hand in his bosom. When he withdrew his hand he found it to be leprous and white as snow (Exod. 4:6). He then followed instructions to repeat the procedure and his hand was healed. The instantaneous recovery was a space-time incident teaching God's power to heal—His power over death and power of life.

The rod-serpent sign suggests God's authority over Satan, the leprous-hand sign, God's power over health, and the water-blood sign, God's power over the provisions of man's needs. It is in these three areas that the miracles of Jesus are applied.

Marah

After only three days' journey from the Red Sea the Israelites were faced with a crisis of survival when the water to which they had come was bitter (Exod. 15:23-26). As the people were desperate they began to murmur, and Moses cried to the Lord;

> *and the Lord showed him a tree; and he threw it into the waters, and the waters became sweet. There He made for them a statute and regulation, and there He*

*tested them. And He said, "If you will give earnest
heed to the voice of the Lord your God, and do what
is right in His sight, and give ear to His command-
ments, and keep all His statutes, I will put none of the
diseases on you which I have put on the Egyptians;
for I, the Lord, am your healer"* (vv. 25-26).

The sweetening of the bitter waters of Marah is associated
with the ordinance of healing that God proceeded to give
Israel. Water is a basic necessity of life and is often used
in Scripture to symbolize the afflictions and judgments that
sin incurs upon humanity as well as the profusion of God's
blessings characterized in the inscrutable providences of
God.

The diseases of the Egyptians, referred to by the Lord,
were familiar to Israel and represent a bitterness which
besets man's lot in life. God's people were to be distinguished, and Marah marked an event—"there He made
for them a statute and regulation, and there He tested
them." Israel was to walk in holy fellowship and obedience
to God; the ordinance and statute were to remind Israel of
God's sovereign provision symbolized by a tree: "For I,
the Lord, am your healer."

The healing tree symbolized the Lord Himself. He alone
can sweeten the bitter vicissitudes of life in the continuous
present, as the last phrase in the Hebrew would imply: "I,
the Lord, am healing you." From this point on, Israel
was to understand that their physical well-being was dependent upon abiding in the redemptive covenant. Protection from disease, as well as healing, was the benefit of the
covenant.

Health and healing in Leviticus

The book of Leviticus is concerned more with the laws

of health than with healing. That God heals His people is not to be treated as an unconditional blessing. But as Israel must walk in fellowship and obedience to God, so Israel must be subservient to principles that govern healthful habits and diets which are part of His creational design.

Health and dietary regulations

Leviticus details a procedure for quarantine which would safeguard the health of Israel (chaps. 13 and 14). Moses by inspiration had received laws of personal cleanliness (chap. 15) unknown to any other people in the ancient world. Many of the laws of hygiene compiled by Moses while under inspiration were not discovered by medical science until modern times.

The Scriptures made diet a matter of holiness among God's covenant people. They, as believers committed to Jehovah, were to care for their bodies by observing faithfully the dietary restrictions placed upon them (chap. 11).

Deuteronomy and the moral law

The final messages of Moses to Israel are called the Second Law, the book of Deuteronomy. God's servant addresses the covenant people on some great issues of spiritual renewal prior to their entrance to the land of promise. Two passages touch on the doctrine of divine healing.

Life in the land of Canaan was to be the highest order of blessing. Israel must understand that God's blessing is conditional. They must keep the terms of the covenant.

Moses warned Israel of the consequences of disobedience to the law.

> *But it shall come about, if you will not obey the Lord your God, to observe to do all His commandments and His statutes which I charge you today, that all these curses shall come upon you and overtake you* (Deut. 28:15).

Just as obedience brought blessing, so disobedience would bring God's curse upon them.

The "curse" in this context should not be thought of in a superstitious sense, for it is an act of God. The "curse" is the retributive judgment upon willful sin in the face of revealed truth. A biblical view of God presents Him as active in judgment as well as in blessing. The curse is the antithesis of blessing. One is as much an act of God as the other.

The Hebrew word *arar* translated "curse" in this passage is the same word used of the curse placed upon the earth by God at the time of the sin of our original parents.

> *Cursed is the ground because of you;*
> *In toil you shall eat of it*
> *All the days of your life.*
> *Both thorns and thistles it shall grow for you;*
> *And you shall eat the plants of the field;*
> *By the sweat of your face*
> *You shall eat bread . . . .* (Gen. 3:17-19).

It is significant that sickness and disease are specifically named as curses upon Israel for their disobedience to God.

> *"The Lord will smite you with consumption and with fever and with inflammation and with fiery heat and with the sword and with blight and with mildew, and they shall pursue you until you perish"* (Deut. 28:22).

> *"The Lord will smite you with the boils of Egypt and with hemorrhoids and with the scab and with the itch, from which you cannot be healed"* (Deut. 28:27).

Eight physical ailments are specified as possible forms the curse of God may take upon those who chose to disobey His moral law. These curses, God said, would not respond to any therapy, thus signifying that the purpose of inflicting the sickness was to get at the underlying spiritual condition.

The second passage on healing in Deuteronomy is in the song of Moses. The man of God, under the inspiration of the Holy Spirit, gives to Israel this psalm describing the dealings of Jehovah with the people who are called by His name. The song is resplendent with revelation about the nature and perfections of God.

> *"See now that I, I am He,*
> *And there is no god besides Me;*
> *It is I who put to death and give life.*
> *I have wounded, and it is I who heal;*
> *And there is no one who can deliver from My hand"*
> (Deut. 32:39).

God is the absolute sovereign, and the scope of His sovereignty includes physical healing. The words of this verse imply that all healing comes under divine sovereignty.

Healing by medical science, by natural process, by diet, or by any other means can never defy the sovereign control of God over men's lives. This truth makes divine healing most reasonable. If God has the last word with regard to healing, why not go to Him first with our physical needs? God is the ultimate Healer.

Moses' vigor

Some consideration should be given to the phenomenon of Moses' physical vitality at an advanced age.

> *Although Moses was one hundred and twenty years old when he died, his eye was not dim nor his vigor abated* (Deut. 34:7).

The careful recording of this fact was not intended as just an unusual human-interest item. The unusual physical strength of the aged Moses has a redemptive history. Moses was strong because of God's touch on his physical life. He needed strength to fulfill the ministry God had given him.

Both Joshua and Caleb enjoyed the same manifestation of God's strength. These examples establish the fact that God by spiritual means can and does impart physical strength to His servants. This concept is more completely developed in the New Testament.

Job and suffering in the blind

The book of Job, though lacking in chronological reference, fits best into the patriarchal era and offers the most complete consideration of the problem of suffering found in the Bible. James said of Job:

> *Behold, we count those blessed who endured. You have heard of the endurance of Job and have seen the outcome of the Lord's dealings, that the Lord is full of compassion and is merciful* (James 5:11).

The message of Job as seen by James was twofold: Job's patience and the Lord's compassion on him. Although the wealthiest man in the East, material possessions had not weaned him from devotion to God. A confrontation in the heavenlies between Satan and God is described.

After Satan returned from one of his excursions the Lord inquired of him, "Have you considered My servant Job? For there is no one like him on the earth, a blameless and upright man, fearing God and turning away from evil" (Job 1:8). Satan retorts that there is no such thing as sincere, disinterested devotion; that everyone forsakes God at a price; and that if he were allowed to touch Job's possessions, Job would renounce God to the face.

Satan is divinely permitted to justify his imputations except for touching Job's own person. Suddenly Job is reduced to extreme poverty, even to the loss of his own children, in four catastrophic events. He is dumbfounded but commits his situation to God and acknowledges the Lord as the giver of every good in life. To God belonged all of Job's rights. He said, "The Lord gave and the Lord has taken away. Blessed be the name of the Lord" (Job 1:21). Job's faith stood fast, and Satan stood discredited.

Satan confronted the Lord with another wager, to allow him to touch Job's person with painful afflictions and this would cause him to curse God to His face (Job 2:5). The Lord accepted the challenge but commanded Satan not to destroy Job. Job is then afflicted with terrible boils over his whole body until he wishes for death that will not come, and his own wife taunts him to curse God and die.

Job is found in the position of penitence on a pile of ashes; he seeks relief by scraping himself with a potsherd. Perhaps the worst suffering was caused by his three friends whose mistaken assumptions and attitudes, explanations and interpretations seem determined to tighten and squeeze Job out of his firm confidence in God.

"Behold, I go forward but He is not there,
And backward, but I cannot perceive Him;

When He acts on the left, I cannot behold Him;
He turns on the right, I cannot see Him.
"But He knows the way I take;
When He has tried me, I shall come forth as gold.
"My foot has held fast to His path;
I have kept His way and not turned aside" (Job 23:8-11).

The greatest lesson of the book is that of trusting God under unknown conditions. Job's life was in God's hands, including his own imperfections (Job 31:33). There are saints who suffer for reasons unknown to them, but they endure in the will of God. They never give up to a fatalistic skepticism but keep their trust in a personal God whose ways are higher than man's ways and continue to look to Him for His deliverance.

Job's story does not end with his struggle. The last chapter is victorious. The contrast is so great that some scholars have called in question its integrity. No evangelical can accept that explanation. Job, chapter 42, is as much the Word of God as the rest of the book, and James emphasizes the outcome of Job's experience. God healed Job while he prayed for his friends; that fact is as important as the experience of suffering Job endured. What encouragement the healing of Job gives to those with chronic, longstanding illnesses.

The Bible reveals that there are times when the best of saints are permitted to suffer, even though God is intimately concerned with their lives. Divine healing is never an end in itself, nor is escapism the reason for the doctrine. Behind every suffering God's purpose is to bless and vindicate the faith of His children.

---

[1]H. C. Leupold, *Exposition of Genesis*, p. 227.

[2]H. C. Leupold, *Exposition of Genesis,* 2:701.

[3]*Ibid,* p. 786.

[4]Franz Delitzsch, *A System of Biblical Psychology,* p. 338.

[5]Douglas J. Harris, *The Biblical Concept of Peace, Shalom,* p. 17.

5

The Period of
the Kings and Prophets

THE COVENANT OF healing Jehovah made with Israel
was not forgotten after the nation settled in the land of
Canaan. The high point in the national life of Israel came
during the reign of Solomon. During this period the boundaries of Israel embraced its largest territories. Under God's
good hand the covenant nation enjoyed an unprecedented
era of prosperity and peace. Among the greatest achieve-
ments of Solomon was the construction of the temple, the
details of which had been given to his father, David, by
divine revelation.

The completion and dedication of the temple marked a
season of spiritual revival for God's people. On the occasion
of dedication, Solomon, under the anointing of the Holy
Spirit, prayed for Israel to enjoy the full scope of redemptive blessing as they faithfully worshiped Jehovah at the
temple.

Solomon's prayer

Solomon's prayer, found in Second Chronicles 6:12-42 and in First Kings 8:22-61, contains a passage imploring healing.

> *"If there is famine in the land, if there is pestilence, if there is blight or mildew, if there is locust or grasshopper, if their enemies besiege them in the land of their cities, whatever plague or whatever sickness there is, whatever prayer or supplication is made by any man or by all Thy people Israel, each knowing his own affliction and his own pain, and spreading his hands toward this house, then hear Thou from heaven Thy dwelling place, and forgive, and render to each according to all his ways, whose heart Thou knowest for Thou alone dost know the hearts of the sons of men, that they may fear Thee, to walk in Thy ways as long as they live in the land which Thou hast given to our fathers"* (2 Chron. 6:28-31).

According to this prayer, when sickness afflicted the individual or large numbers of people in Israel they were to resort to prayer. The qualifying terms resemble those laid down at the waters of Marah when Jehovah first revealed Himself as healer to the nation. Forgiveness attended physical recovery.

It can be implied from Solomon's words that healing as a covenant benefit received through prayer was still understood in Israel in Solomon's time. His father, David, was no stranger to this truth. The Psalms of David contain a theology of healing. Solomon had no doubt reflected many times on the promises of physical healing contained in the Scripture existent in that day. His own proverbs reveal an in-depth understanding of the doctrine of healing.

The Psalms

The Psalms always speak of healing as the privilege of the believer in a redemptive context. The reflective student becomes aware of a deep language of the soul in these ancient songs and the psychology of mind regarding physical healing. The disturbed state of mind that often attends sickness and the various stages of mental attitude the experience of pain and disease brings are easily detected.

The sixth Psalm provides a good example of the state of mind frequently found in the sick. Fear, dismay, and an uncontrolled emotional state plagued the psalmist, but as he lifted his need to God in prayer a change took place in his attitudes; healing brought to his troubled heart prepared the way for physical healing.

David on one occasion was healed from a fatal illness in answer to prayer. Psalm 30 records his song of thanksgiving to God.

> *O Lord my God,*
> *I cried to Thee for help, and Thou didst heal me.*
> *O Lord, Thou hast brought up my soul from Sheol;*
> *Thou hast kept me alive, that I should not go down to*
>   *the pit.*
> *Sing praise to the Lord, you His godly ones,*
> *And give thanks to His holy name* (vv. 2-4).

One senses the struggle David endured as he sensed his life was slipping away. His prayer was a cry of desperation for God's intervention. Saints have often experienced healing at the very gates of death. The fact that the physical condition has deteriorated to the point of no human hope ought not deter prayer for recovery.

The most theological statement about healing in the book of Psalms is in the 103d.

> *Bless the Lord, O my soul;*
> *And all that is within me, bless His holy name.*
> *Bless the Lord, O my soul,*
> *And forget none of His benefits;*
> *Who pardons all your iniquities;*
> *Who heals all your diseases;*
> *Who redeems your life from the pit;*
> *Who crowns you with lovingkindness and compassion;*
> *Who satisfies your years with good things,*
> *So that your youth is renewed like the eagle* (vv. 1-5).

The healing of the body from disease is listed as a benefit of redemption. The blessing of healing includes recovery from disease, deliverance from the grave, and renewal of physical vigor. David makes the strong statement that he was redeemed from the ultimate outcome of his sickness. This certainly suggests that David thought of divine healing as being in the atonement.

Psalm 107 is a series of admonitions urging saints to give God the glory for having triumphed over their difficulties. Among the triumphs of faith is recovery from illness. They were so sick as to desire no food. As they drew near to the time of death, they cried to God and He saved them. The direct means of healing in this case was the Word of God.

> *He sent His word and healed them* (v. 20).

Christ often healed by His "word." The "word" was a word of command. God speaking in divine sovereignty commanded, and the healing was immediately effected.

The Hebrew word *rapha* is used seven times in the Psalms. Four of these passages refer to physical healing; three, to healing in the spiritual sense of correcting a spiritual condition. It is clear that David and other writers of the hymns of Israel understood the blessing of divine healing.

The Proverbs

The Proverbs have been referred to as heavenly advice for earthly living. They touch real-life situations, familiar to every man, with wisdom from above. The admonitions given in this book by divine revelation are designed for practice in holy living.

The subject of health and healing emerges several times in the Proverbs. They show the direct bearing of a proper mental attitude on physical well-being. They also show the effect one's spiritual condition may have on his state of health.

The Bible teaches not a mind-over-matter concept so common to the cults, but a relationship between mental and physical health. The mind has no innate power to cure, but a sound mind has a wholesome effect on the whole personality. Healthy thinking promotes a healthy body.

Solomon wrote:

> *Do not be wise in your own eyes;*
> *Fear the Lord and turn away from evil.*
> *It will be healing to your body,*
> *And refreshment to your bones* (Prov. 3:7-8).

The virtue of humility, a wholesome reverence for God, and a persistent refusal of the ways of sin describe a condition of heart conducive to physical healing. A by-product of doing right is physical refreshment. The believer who chooses the right consistently is free of much of the frustration characteristic of modern people.

Anxiety is a major factor in the high rate of mental and physical illness prevalent in modern society. The follower of Christ is subject to anxiety just as the non-Christian. The believer must learn to think with a Christian mind, or he will succumb to anxiety along with those who do not know Christ. The indwelling Spirit seeks to teach each believer the secret of inner peace. Resistance to the dealings of the Spirit often accounts for the troubled minds of many Christians. When all known sin is confessed internal conflicts are resolved, and quietness and peace bring healing to the mind.

The thought life is associated with the emotional life of the believer. Streams of poison flow into the system when he is overcome with unhealthy emotions aggravated by unhealthy thoughts. Anger can produce serious physical side effects. Envy can cripple the soul and sicken the body. Depression eats away at the whole personality with devastating effect.

Healthy emotions are the fruits of a Spirit-controlled life. They lift and bless man in spirit, soul, and body.

> *A tranquil heart is life to the body,*
> *But passion is rottenness to the bones* (Prov. 14:30).

> *A joyful heart is good medicine,*
> *But a broken spirit dries up the bones* (17:22).

> *The spirit of a man can endure his sickness,*
> *But a broken spirit who can bear?* (18:14)

Far ahead of his time Solomon learned by revelation health secrets that modern medicine has only recently discovered. The believer does well to read Proverbs often, implanting these concepts firmly in his thought and training his habits of reaction to circumstances. The government of man's spirit has much to do with his total well-being.

Proverbs 4:20-22 is a key passage on the doctrine of healing:

My son, give attention to my words;
Incline your ear to my sayings.
Do not let them depart from your sight;
Keep them in the midst of your heart.
For they are life to those who find them,
And health to all their whole body.

This passage points out how important it is for the believer to retain the Word of God in his mind. Constant
exposure to the wisdom of God as given in the Word is
man's best medicine, for it ministers health to the whole
body.

Jeroboam—the paralyzed hand

An unnamed prophet of God from Judah was commissioned to warn Jeroboam, the founder and king of Israel,
of his sins (1 Kings 13:1-10). Upon his arrival at Bethel the
prophet confronted Jeroboam as he was about to make
sacrifice at his pagan altar set up in defiance of separation
from Judah. The prophet not only denounced the pagan
altar but commanded a sign, that the altar would split
apart and the ashes on it would spill to the ground.

Jeroboam in anger shouted to his guards to arrest the
man and shook his fist at him; as he did, his arm became
paralyzed in that position and the altar was rent. The king
pled with the prophet to pray that his arm might be restored. The prophet prayed and God healed the arm.

King Jeroboam was deeply moved and he offered the
prophet a reward, but his heart remained unchanged. Signs
and miracles in themselves will never turn the hearts of unbelievers.

Jeroboam's son Abijah

Later, Abijah, the son of Jeroboam, was stricken with

illness (1 Kings 14) and the disturbed father devised a scheme to learn of his son's fate. God forewarned the prophet Ahijah of Jeroboam's plan. When Jeroboam's disguised wife appeared, the prophet addressed her with the sad news that Abijah would die, and then said, "And all Israel shall mourn for him and bury him, for he alone of Jeroboam's family shall come to the grave, because in him something good was found toward the Lord God of Israel in the house of Jeroboam" (1 Kings 14:13).

Evidently, death by this sickness was an act of mercy because of the judgment that would come upon Jeroboam (v. 10). God in His sovereignty chose to heal the arm of Jeroboam but not Abijah because of the good that was found in him. God's value system and knowledge of the future are principles that enter into God's sovereign working, but this ought not to deter earnest prayer and the exercise of faith. Despite Jeroboam's departure from the Lord, he knew God had the power of life and of death.

Elijah and the widow's son

During Elijah's ministry, the raising of the son of the widow of Zarephath was the only healing miracle. This event, described in First Kings 17:17-24, should not be confused with resurrection. The Scriptures indicate that those raised from the dead in both the Old and New Testaments retained their mortal bodies and were subject to death as other men. Notice the language of verses 21-22:

> *Then he . . . called to the Lord, and said, "O Lord my God, I pray Thee, let this child's life return to him." And the Lord heard the voice of Elijah, and the life of the child returned to him and he revived.*

The raising of this widow's son was a healing, not a resurrection. God can quicken or revitalize the body; the raising of a person from death is next to actual resurrection which is a permanent state—the ultimate in healing power.

We, in our faith, are usually conditioned by the apparent possibilities before us, but God is not. Even Jesus prayed in Gethsemane, "Abba (Father), all things are possible for Thee; remove this cup from Me; yet not what I will, but what Thou wilt" (Mark 14:36). It was not God's will and Jesus died, but this does not mean Jesus should not have prayed as He did. In answer to the prayer of Elijah, "the life of the child returned to him and he revived."

Healing in Second Kings

The low spiritual level of God's covenant people during the closing years of the divided kingdom is graphically described in Second Kings. Still, eight passages relate to physical healing; God's remnant was looking to Jehovah-*rapha*. The healing sciences had not been developed; Israel looked either to the Lord for healing or, their alternative, to evil spirits, which greatly displeased God.

Ahaziah's fatal mistake

Ahaziah, the king of Israel, had a serious accident when he "fell through the lattice in his upper chamber which was in Samaria" (2 Kings 1:2). Being seriously ill, he sent messengers to inquire of Baal-zebub, the god of Ekron. Then Elijah was sent by God to meet these messengers and to say: "Is it because there is no God in Israel that you are going to inquire of Baal-zebub, the god of Ekron? Now therefore thus says the Lord, 'You shall not come down from the bed where you have gone up, but you shall surely die'" (vv. 3-4).

As long as Israel held a true view of God as He had revealed Himself to them, it was common procedure to turn to the Lord in sickness—this is what the Lord expected of His people. Ahaziah's refusal of the light he had been given brought a stern rebuke from the Lord as a testimony to all Israel.

That God had made a covenant with Israel and had revealed Himself as Jehovah-*rapha* was a matter not of feeling or religious inclination, but of fact even as God's judgment upon Ahaziah became historical fact. The experiences of people who were not healed in Second Kings are as significant as those who were healed because healing is treated as part and parcel of God's redemptive provision.

Elisha and the Shunammite woman's son

A woman from Shunem and her husband opened their home to the prophet Elisha and prepared a special chamber with furnishings to accommodate him (2 Kings 4:10). After Elisha and his servant Gehazi experienced this hospitality several times, Elisha offered to speak to the king or to the captain of the army concerning a form of reward for this kind couple. The woman, however, brushed the offer with the words, "I live among my own people."

Gehazi observed to the prophet that the woman had no son and that her husband was old. Elisha then commanded Gehazi to call the woman; as she stood at the threshold of Elisha's door he said to her, "At this season next year you shall embrace a son." She was touched by God's healing hand and bore a son at the time predicted by Elisha.

Years later, the boy born of a miracle suffered a stroke in the harvest field and was brought home where he died

(v. 20). The Shunammite woman carried her dead son to Elisha's bed, closed the door, and went to find Elisha. Elisha immediately commanded Gehazi to run ahead and to lay his staff on the lad's face.

But Elisha's instructions brought no results. When Elisha arrived he entered the chamber and closed the door in privacy with the boy. A struggle of prayer, patience, and persistence ensued. The prophet stretched his own body on the boy, placed his mouth to the boy's mouth, and eventually the boy sneezed and opened his eyes.

There are several points of interest in this account. The woman believed God and persisted in honoring the prophet as a servant of God. Elisha was faced with a crisis of faith and the apparent necessity of full identification with the lifeless body of the boy in travail before God's presence alone. Mere methods of procedure did not avail but faith in the vicarious life God provides brought victory.

Naaman the leper

The most unusual healing of the divided kingdom period was the recovery of a Gentile army officer through the ministry of Elisha (2 Kings 5). Naaman, the captain of the army of Syria, had so distinguished himself that he had won the respect not only of the king, but of the commoner on the street. But the disease of leprosy had attacked Naaman and his whole career was in jeopardy.

Among the household servants to Naaman was an Israelite girl captured in war. She had learned to love and respect Naaman and was grieved over the fate that apparently faced him. One day she dared to share with her mistress that the God of Israel healed the sick and suggested that he see Elisha the prophet whose power in prayer was well known.

Naaman was given a letter from the king of Syria together with a lavish royal reward, and he went to see the king of Israel rather than the prophet as the Israelite damsel had suggested. Upon receiving the letter, the king of Israel became angry and tore his clothes. Assuming that the king of Syria was seeking an occasion for a quarrel, he said, "Am I God, to kill and to make alive, that this man is sending word to me to cure a man of his leprosy?"

Hearing of the predicament Elisha sent word to send the captain of the Syrian army to him that he might know there was a prophet in Israel. When Naaman arrived a servant from Elisha met him with the abrupt instruction that he should wash seven times in the Jordan and he would be healed.

All the pride of Naaman's heart rebelled. It had been humiliating enough to be misinterpreted by the king with the offer of ten talents of silver, six thousand pieces of gold, and ten changes of raiment. But to be met by the prophet's servant instead of by the prophet and to be told to dip seven times in the muddy waters of the Jordan without formal greeting or an opportunity to offer gifts—that was too much!

> *Naaman was furious and went away and said, "Behold, I thought, 'He will surely come out to me, and stand and call on the name of the Lord his God, and wave his hand over the place, and cure the leper.' Are not Abanah and Pharpar, the rivers of Damascus, better than all the waters of Israel? Could I not wash in them and be clean?" So he turned and went away in a rage* (vv. 11-12).

Fortunately his servants persuaded him not to react so strongly. They said, "My father, had the prophet told you to do some great thing, would you not have done it? How much more then, when he says to you, 'Wash, and be clean'?'' (v. 13)

Reluctantly, Naaman and his party went to the Jordan. Seven dips in the river and Naaman was a well man. Elisha knew by the Spirit's illumination that primarily Naaman needed to recognize God and not necessarily the prophet, that God's working is not to be bargained for but is possible by faith in humble obedience. Pride, anger, rebellion, and prejudice block the blessing of God.

Jesus referred to this occurrence in Luke 4:27:

> *"And there were many lepers in Israel in the time of Elisha the prophet; and none of them was cleansed, but only Naaman the Syrian."*

Christ was rebuking the unbelief of the people of His home town, Nazareth, with the inference that had obedience been more common in Elisha's day, healing would have been more frequent.

That God's way of answering prayer is not to be trifled with is depicted in the greedy desire of Gehazi, Elisha's servant, to benefit from the gifts Naaman had brought with him (2 Kings 5:20-27). His scheming plot after Naaman was healed was rewarded with the very leprosy of which Naaman had been cured.

Hezekiah's sickness

At the peak of his illustrious reign over the southern kingdom, Hezekiah was smitten with a fatal illness. God told the prophet Isaiah to warn the king that he should prepare for death. The facts relating to his healing are so important that they are recorded three times in the Old Testament (2 Kings 20:1-7; 2 Chron. 32:24-31; Isa. 38:1-22). Each account provides some important detail omitted in the others and differs from the others in perspective.

King Hezekiah was healed in answer to his own intense prayer to God. The content of his prayer, or at least that portion which has been preserved in Scripture, is important. The king did not seek God's will for his life, but insisted that he be healed.

However, it appears that Hezekiah's motivations were pure. He sought healing that he might continue to minister to Judah, God's people. Hezekiah's prayer seems to indicate that the basis of his petition was the kind of man he had been and the service he had rendered. However, Second Kings 20:3 could have a deeper meaning:

> *"Remember now, O Lord, I beseech Thee, how I have walked before Thee in truth and with a whole heart, and have done what is good in Thy sight."*

If this prayer is laid alongside Exodus 15:26, a quite different interpretation becomes obvious. Was it the purpose of Hezekiah to remind God of his goodness or to remind God of the terms of the covenant? Jehovah had promised:

> *"If you will give earnest heed to the voice of the Lord your God, and do what is right in His sight, and give ear to His commandments, and keep all His statutes, I will put none of these diseases on you which I have put on the Egyptians; for I, the Lord, am your healer."*

Hezekiah must surely have had in mind this covenant of healing as the basis of his plea for healing.

The language of Scripture in Hezekiah's prayer indicates something very human about the king. He showed no pretense regarding his feelings and state of mind on learning that he had a terminal illness, but wept bitterly as he turned his face to the wall in an act of human despair. The beautiful Hymn of Healing composed by Hezekiah upon his recovery in a very sensitive way describes his deep human struggle for faith before the answer came:

> *"Like a swallow, like a crane, so I twitter;*
> *I moan like a dove;*
> *My eyes look wistfully to the heights;*
> *O Lord, I am oppressed, be my security"* (Isa. 38:14).

Those who minister to the sick ought not to be impatient if the suffering one struggles with fear and emotional upheaval, but should keep praying and believing.

A part of Hezekiah's victory may be attributed to a legitimate love for life.

> *"O Lord, by these things men live;*
> *And in all these is the life of my spirit;*
> *O restore me to health, and let me live!"* (v. 16)

The psalmist said:

> *Who is the man who desires life,*
> *And loves length of days that he may see good?*
> *Keep your tongue from evil,*
> *And your lips from speaking deceit.*
> *Depart from evil, and do good;*
> *Seek peace, and pursue it* (34:12-14).

These verses were a part of Hezekiah's Bible. He used this biblical principle as the ground of his petition for physical healing. God's Word had taught him to love a good life. That good life was enjoyed by only those who walked in the righteous precepts of Jehovah God.

A shadow falls on the beautiful story of King Hezekiah's healing. The writer of Second Chronicles summarizes Hezekiah's fault in one brief verse:

> *But Hezekiah gave no return for the benefit he received, because his heart was proud; therefore wrath came on him and on Judah and Jerusalem* (32:25).

Isaiah gives another insight into Hezekiah's selfish attitude. The prophet announced the total destruction of Hezekiah's house and captivity in the land of Babylon because of the foolishness and pride the king had displayed when certain ambassadors from Babylon had come to congratulate him on his recovery. To this Hezekiah replied, " 'The word of the Lord which you have spoken is good.' For he thought, 'For there will be peace and truth in my days' " (39:8).

It is amazing that even though Hezekiah knew he had only another fifteen years to live, according to the prophet's earlier word (38:5), after physical vigor and good health were restored, his spiritual life deteriorated rather than improved. God was sovereign over Hezekiah's length of days and the miracle of deliverance from a chastening sickness did not meet his inmost need.

The experience of Hezekiah serves as a warning to all who enjoy God's healing touch in their bodies. A healed body should be presented as a vessel wholly for God's use and every self-interest should be crucified. Hezekiah did not lose his healing, but he lost his anointing, a far greater loss.

Isaiah's gospel

The writing prophets of the Old Testament make frequent mention of the redemptive healing Jehovah provides for His people. Isaiah more than any other prophet speaks of physical healings, in particular. As an eyewitness to the remarkable healing of King Hezekiah, he carefully details the story, preserving the psalm of healing composed by the king after his health was restored (38:9-20).

The writings of Isaiah have sometimes been called the "gospel" of the Old Testament because of their content.

By means of the inspiration of the Holy Spirit, Isaiah saw Christ and presented His ministry and death centuries in advance. He clearly saw Christ as the healer. He proclaimed that Messiah's kingdom would be attended by the healing of the sick and that Zion would know release from sickness.

> *And no resident will say, "I am sick"* (33:24).

Isaiah described the glorious days of Christ:

> *Then the eyes of the blind will be opened,*
> *And the ears of the deaf will be unstopped.*
> *Then the lame will leap like a deer,*
> *And the tongue of the dumb will shout for joy* (35:5-6a).

> *"Behold, My Servant, whom I uphold;*
> *My chosen one in whom My soul delights.*
> *I have put My Spirit upon him;*
>
> *To open blind eyes"* (42:1, 7a).

Christ Himself, when reading in the synagogue at Nazareth from Isaiah 61—a passage similar to 35:5-6—about His anointing for ministry, added the phrase, from 42:7, *to open blind eyes* (recorded in Luke 4:17-19).

Isaiah saw Calvary through the Spirit of prophecy and put down in writing a perfect description of the agonies which Christ suffered in His death. The Holy Spirit revealed to Isaiah, in chapter 53, that the sufferings of Christ were related to bodily healing as well as to spiritual healing. This chapter is twice quoted in the New Testament as having reference to Christ.

Because the theological implications of these verses have been considered in chapter two, it is sufficient to point out that Isaiah included physical infirmity in the vicarious death of Christ and recognized physical healing as a benefit of spiritual overflow.

The Holy Spirit enabled Isaiah to write of Israel's future restoration. His particular emphasis is on her spiritual recovery. Isaiah saw that in the day Israel truly repents and gives herself to Jehovah God, great spiritual blessings will come to the covenant nation:

> *"Then your light will break out like the dawn,*
> *And your recovery will speedily spring forth;*
> *And your righteousness will go before you;*
> *The glory of the Lord will be your rear guard"* (58:8).

The spiritual "explosion" in a clean heart has its side effects in the whole being, including the physical.

Daniel—Nebuchadnezzar's mental illness

The book of Daniel preserves the record of a remarkable healing of mental illness.

Nebuchadnezzar, the powerful king of Babylon, had been exposed to the true faith by the exiles from Judah. Daniel and three other young Hebrews held responsible positions in his government; the reality of their faith in Jehovah had reached the king, but pride prevented him from embracing the true God.

God's message of warning to Nebuchadnezzar came by means of a dream which Daniel interpreted for him but which he chose to ignore (Dan. 4). Though he was the world's mightiest king in his day, God providentially took away his reason. For seven years he was a helpless incompetent, imitating an animal, even as Daniel had predicted in the interpretation of the dream.

At the end of that period of seven years, God touched him and his reason returned. Whether or not the prayers and ministries of those believers in the king's court had been used to effect this healing is not recorded.

Either by human instrumentality—or without it—this healing was an act of divine sovereignty. This proud pagan king, humbled by God's direct intervention in his life, became a believer, as his testimony attests.

Nebuchadnezzar's healing offers encouragement to those seeking help for mental illness. Though he lived in this hopeless condition for seven years, the Lord's healing completely restored him to normal life (Dan. 4:37). God can heal the mind as well as the body!

Jeremiah's prophecy of Israel's recovery

It is Jeremiah who speaks prophetically of healing. The weeping prophet laments the ruin of Zion and cries for her restoration. He sees the recovery of the covenant people to be more than political and national—Zion will revive because God redeems her.

The mental state of the prophet is seen in chapter 8:

> *Because the Lord our God has doomed us*
> *And given us poisoned water to drink,*
> *For we have sinned against the Lord.*
> *We waited for peace, but no good came;*
> *For a time of healing, but behold, terror!* (vv. 14b-15)

Zion's recovery is to be a "time of healing" in the broadest sense of that phrase. Zion is to be mended and made whole.

It is customary to interpret such references as having to do entirely with the spiritual blessings of Zion. But all of the descriptions of that glad day include much more than spiritual blessing. In the kingdom days, Zion will be healed politically, socially, economically, physically, and spiritually!

Jeremiah's references to redemptive healing must surely include health for the people of God:

> *" 'For I will restore you to health*
> *And I will heal you of your wounds,' declares the*
> *   Lord"* (30:17a).

> *"Behold, I will bring to it health and healing, and I*
> *will heal them; and I will reveal to them an abundance*
> *of peace and truth"* (33:6).

Ezekiel's parallel to Jeremiah

Ezekiel clearly associates healing even more with the day of Israel's regathering. He rebukes the pastors of Israel for their neglect of the sick and the diseased (Ezek. 34:4).

Because the "shepherds" could not be trusted, Jehovah Himself will take up the care of His sheep in that day. He determines to bring them back to the place of blessing. Jehovah will also be their healer, binding up their wounds and strengthening their sick (v. 16).

Malachi's prophecy of Messiah as Healer

The last chapter of Malachi, the last book of the Old Testament, announces that the Messiah will be the Healer as He comes into the world.

> *"The sun of righteousness will rise with healing in its*
> *wings; and you will go forth and skip about like calves*
> *from the stall"* (4:2b).

Christ was Healer when He ministered on this earth scene in the days of His flesh. He is Healer now enthroned in heaven above, but continues to act on earth through His church. Christ will be Healer in the day of His coming when He returns to set up His kingdom and rule over the nations of the earth.

On whatever age the rays of the Sun of Righteousness may fall there will be healing in His wings. The coming kingdom age will be no exception. The prophets seem to speak with one voice of that "time of healing" in the days of the public manifestation of Christ's reign over the nations. During that coming time, man will enjoy physical health unequaled in any other period of history since the fall.

Conclusion

The truth of divine healing is a part of the theology of the Old Testament. The historical, the poetical, and the prophetic books—all teach healing for the saints.

Young's Analytical Concordance lists 154 references to healing in the Bible. The most frequent Hebrew word is *rapha,* occurring 56 times in the Old Testament. *Rapha* has the root meaning of "to bind or sew together," to heal in the sense of repairing the physical condition. The context would verify that at least one-half of the passages using *rapha* have references to physical rather than spiritual healing.

The four other Hebrew words which are translated "healing" in English versions of the Bible are *marpe, kehah, tealah,* and *nathan rephuoth.*

The Old Testament Scriptures teach the same basic doctrine of physical healing as the New Testament teaches. In summary, there are eight aspects of the doctrine of divine healing presented in the Old Testament.

1. The Old Testament projects a definition of health as the well-being of the whole man.

2. The origin of sickness is traced to man's fall. The

immediate cause of sickness may or may not be the result of specific sin.

3. The Old Testament reveals God as having the office of Healer.

4. The blessing of physical healing was given Israel as a part of her covenant relationship to Jehovah.

5. Many passages of the Old Testament present prayer as the means by which physical healing came.

6. Health is presented as more important than healing. Practical guidelines on diet, sanitation, and the isolation of infectious disease were given by God to His people for their health.

7. The historical portions of the Old Testament contain specific examples of physical healing by divine intervention.

8. The Old Testament teaches the quickening of the body through the immediate ministry of the Holy Spirit.

6

The Healing Christ

ACROSS THE CENTURIES the spirit of prophecy had
been announcing the coming of God's anointed One.
Prophets taught Old Testament saints that healing power
would be one of the credentials of the Christ of God.

When the fullness of time arrived the eternal Christ
stepped out of heaven and took on human form and lived
in our world. The Gospel records were inspired by the
Holy Spirit to give a reliable account of the birth, the life,
the work, the death, and the resurrection of the Incarnate
Son of God.

The reason for Christ's healing ministry

A survey tracing the healing ministry of the Lord Jesus
Christ while He was in the flesh and upon earth begins
this study of healing in the New Testament. There can be
no question that Jesus, born in Bethlehem, was the very
Son of God and the Jehovah-*rapha* of the Old Testament.

The Healer was now incarnate and upon earth.

The question to be answered in order to keep His healing ministry in proper perspective is, Why did Jesus perform many bodily healings? Bible scholars seem to take a common position that healing was exclusively a credential of deity—a validation that Jesus was the very Son of God. True, the miracles did offer proof that Christ was indeed God in the flesh. However, the New Testament Scriptures offer other explanations for His healing ministry.

Peter, when preaching in the house of Cornelius, made this remarkable statement:

> *You know of Jesus of Nazareth, how God anointed Him with the Holy Spirit and with power, and how He went about doing good, and healing all who were oppressed by the devil; for God was with Him* (Acts 10:38).

Peter indicates that the healing ministry of the Lord Jesus was an act of goodness on the part of the Savior. Matthew, on at least two occasions, mentions compassion as Christ's motivation for acts of healing.

One cannot read of the healing of the servant's ear that had been cut off by Peter on the occasion of the confrontation in the garden just prior to Jesus' arrest without sensing the tenseness of that scene. Peter, filled with violence and fear, feeling that he must do something to help Christ, in one impetuous act cut off the servant's ear. At that point, when most men would have been too confused to act intelligently, the Incarnate Son of God quietly picked up the ear, placed it to the side of the head of Malchus, and instantly healed him.

This evidence of an act of mercy indicates that the healing ministry of Christ cannot be treated solely as proof of deity or of the supernatural. It must be treated also as an expression of the mercy, compassion, and goodness of His pure and perfect heart. To heal was natural for the Lord Jesus.

> The healing miracles indicate that Jesus came to redeem, but they are more than symbols of redemption, they are in themselves part of His redemptive work.[1]

The concrete reality of Christ's healings

Most commentaries treat the healing incidents as if they were merely types or symbols of spiritual truth. For generations this faulty interpretation has blinded most of the Christian community to vital truth regarding divine healing for the body. Evangelicals who are most enthusiastic for the literal interpretation of Old Testament prophecy will abandon this method in the treatment of the Gospel records that are obviously historical in nature.

Henry B. Wilson wrote:

> The miracles were great literal facts, hard facts, which had to do with the physical world and the physical side of man's nature. Great facts which reveal the existence of spiritual laws and the wonderful results of their effect upon the material and physical plane in proportion to man's faith and his cooperation with the will of God.[2]

It must be admitted that Jesus Christ actually healed physical maladies during His earthly ministry. It must be admitted also that the church enjoyed the ministry of healing subsequent to Christ's ascension to heaven and the outpouring of the Holy Spirit. Spiritualizing the healings of Christ will not explain the phenomenon of healing.

The Bible student must deal first with the plain sense of the Scripture text, observing every detail of data with care. What kind of people did Jesus heal? Did He always use the same method? Were conditions laid down for healing?

Were there factors that hindered or helped healing? Did Christ ever associate physical healing with an individual spiritual condition? By answering these questions the primary meaning can be discovered. Devotional thoughts are often secondary meanings, never to be substituted for the primary meaning.

Principles to be observed in Christ's healing ministry

The healing of the impotent man at the pool of Bethesda (John 5:1-9) is an example of this devotional type of interpretation. Most commentators give many pages of material on this incident. They may include an exegesis of the Greek text and some devotional thoughts on the story, but not one word regarding the ability and the power of Jesus Christ to heal the sick. Their exposition ignores the primary meaning of the text.

The miracles recorded in the Gospel of John receive the same treatment by most commentators. It is true that John selected, under the guidance of the Holy Spirit, healings and miracles with the express purpose of validating the deity of Christ, but the fact that he includes details as to the means by which the individuals received healing indicates that these cases had broader significance. That they offer instruction for those who seek Christ's healing touch can be justly claimed.

Christ's compassion

Of the thirty-five miracles performed by Christ, as recorded in the four Gospels, twenty-eight fall in the category of bodily or mental healing. That much of the supernatural ministry of the Lord Jesus Christ should be de-

voted to healing is most significant. The miracles of Christ
were not promotional items, but were deliberately designed
compassionate acts to relieve human suffering. They are
an index to the very heart of God.

As we picture the Lord Jesus Christ moving among the
multitudes, relieving their physical ills, we learn of His
holy and compassionate disposition. We learn of His love
for man and of His desire to relieve man from the effects
of sin. Christ's role as healer was a redemptive ministry,
not merely a dispensational one. No limitations were placed
on His healing ministry on earth. Unbelief was the only
recorded hindrance to healing.

All case histories in the Gospels deal with real and difficult physical conditions. The following diseases or conditions are mentioned:

epilepsy	hemorrhage
leprosy	dropsy
paralysis	dumbness
fever	lameness
blindness	withered hand

Obviously, Jesus exercised His mighty power to deal
with serious fatal diseases and conditions of the human
body. His healing ministry was not a charlatan's trickery
to bring release to those with minor nervous disorders.
The Lord Jesus Christ was, and is, a legitimate healer because He is God, and God has no limitations on His power.

Christ's character

Never is the power of God in healing or in any other
miracle displayed in isolation from the moral qualities of
His person. Archbishop Trench, in his remarkable book
on miracles, wrote:

Each true miracle will always be more or less redemptive acts.

In other words, works not merely of power but of grace, each one an index and a prophecy of the inner work of man's deliverance, which it accompanies and helps forward. . . . It was preeminently thus with the miracles of Christ. There was nothing stereotyped about the healing ministry of Christ. Each case history has its own special features. They deserve very careful study for they contain a wealth of basic principles for those who would seek the healing Christ today. Throughout the earthly ministry of the Lord Jesus He observed a respect for human individuality. He was very sensitive to the particular and individual needs of those who came to Him seeking physical help. This fact alone would account for many of the variations in methodology employed by Christ. The particular method employed was dictated by the condition of the seeker. This can be very well illustrated in the case of the blind man healed at Bethsaida. The scriptural account is in Mark 8:22-25.

> And they came to Bethsaida, and they brought a blind man to him and entreated him to touch him. And taking the blind man by the hand he brought him out of the village and after spitting on his eyes and laying his hands upon him he asked him, "Do you see anything?" and he looked up and said, "I see men for I am seeing them like trees walking about." Then again he laid his hands upon his eyes, and he looked intently and was restored and began to see everything clearly.[3]

Trench suggests that the Lord Jesus detected a lack of spiritual understanding in this man and, therefore, He chose to veil the miraculous by use of spittle. He further accommodated Himself to the man's condition by dealing with his illness progressively. Many claim that unless a healing is instantaneous, it is not a healing at all, but the distinctive mark of this miracle is that the Lord Jesus, in this instance, chose to heal gradually.

The question of sin

Christ did not hesitate to relate sickness to man's condition of sin, as shown in the account of the paralytic brought to the Lord Jesus (Mark 2:3 ff.). When Christ saw the man's condition, His first word to him was, "My son, your sins are forgiven." Immediately some of the scribes were alarmed; they incisively recognized the claim of position Christ was making for Himself.

> *Jesus, perceiving in His spirit that they were reasoning that way within themselves, said to them, "Why are you reasoning about these things in your hearts? Which is easier, to say to the paralytic, 'Your sins are forgiven'; or to say, 'Arise, and take up your pallet and walk'? But in order that you may know that the Son of Man has authority on earth to forgive sins"— He said to the paralytic, "I say to you, rise, take up your pallet and go home" (vv. 8-11).*

It is contrary to the nature of Christ to give what is not desired, but Jesus understood the man and the quest of his inmost soul; He called the paralytic "son" and relieved him of a misery worse than physical ailment. Jesus Christ is Lord and Provider of both spiritual and physical needs, but the spiritual is first and foremost. The paralytic was not an approved candidate for healing until after the sin question was settled.

Though many who were unaware of their sin problem were healed, here was a candidate for the fuller blessing. James associates faith for healing with the need of forgiveness among believers in the church:

> *Is anyone among you sick? Let him call for the elders of the church, and let them pray over him, anointing him with oil in the name of the Lord; and the prayer offered in faith will restore the one who is sick, and the Lord will raise him up, and if he has committed*

> *sins, they will be forgiven him. Therefore, confess your sins to one another, and pray for one another, so that you may be healed. The effective prayer of a righteous man can accomplish much (5:14-16).*

The threshold of faith for healing is coincident with a conscious fellowship with God and the church in regard to the believer—it is part of the "children's bread." Though multitudes through the inscrutable ways of God were healed by signs and wonders and who nevertheless continued in their sin, the sin problem for the believer is of another kind.

Whether the paralytic was "accepted" of God as a ready candidate for the gospel light, or whether he had failed God specifically in known sin as a believer—as seems most likely—may be debatable, but the crux of his need remained the same: sin was to be dealt with before the physical benefit of healing was bestowed. Jesus did not act simply to accommodate the need of the scribes, He acted in accordance with His character and will.

In one of Christ's visits to Jerusalem He came upon a man in the crowd that waited day after day at the pool of Bethesda, a man who had been thirty-eight years in a crippled condition.

> *When Jesus saw him lying there, and knew that he had already been a long time in that condition, He said to him, "Do you wish to get well?" The sick man answered Him, "Sir, I have no man to put me into the pool when the water is stirred up, but while I am coming, another steps down before me." Jesus said to him, "Arise, take up your pallet, and walk." And immediately the man became well, and took up his pallet and began to walk (John 5:6-9).*

Jesus, finding him in the temple some time later, said,

"Behold, you have become well; do not sin any more,
so that nothing worse may befall you" (v. 14).

At last the condition of sin that had bound this man had
been broken. Out of the multitudes of sick (v. 3) at the
pool Jesus singled out this one whose expression to Him
for healing brought not only physical but also spiritual
wholeness. Christ warned him that he should walk in the
new life of holiness and devotion, so that a worse judgment would not come upon his life.

Interesting, is it not, that the Scripture does not tell
us what the sin of this sick man had been. But *he* knew
full well what his sin was, and he took to heart the Savior's
exhortation to forsake it unreservedly that he might continue to be whole in spirit, soul, and body.

Faith for healing

Not to be overlooked is Jesus' initial question: "Do you
wish to get well?" Apparently the years of waiting had
brought deadness, unbelief, and withdrawal into the experience of this man—so deep that Christ dealt with this
before attempting to touch his physical condition. Scripture demonstrates that Jesus Christ, by virtue of His deity,
could heal any physical malady quite apart from the spiritual condition, but normally the Savior chose to heal upon
response from the seeker, and the principal response was
that of faith.

Christ had a way of awakening faith in the hearts of
those who had need. The case of the man with the withered
hand (Mark 3:1 ff.) is a good example.

It is difficult to imagine the kind of mental suffering
this man had endured. He may have been a craftsman, and
some accident caused his hand to be withered and useless.

In any event, the condition brought limitations upon his life.

Apparently Christ sensed a lack of faith and understanding. He began to draw out the man's faith, first, by an invitation to rise and come to Him. Then the man, listening to Jesus' words to the Pharisees who were there to oppose His ministry, sensed that Jesus was about to do something good. His faith was born at the moment Jesus said, "Stretch out your hand." Christ called for a demonstration of obedience.

The Gospels record a number of healings when Christ asked for obedience from those who sought His help. There cannot be true faith without obedience. Oftentimes unwillingness to obey in an issue clearly pointed out by the Spirit of God is a hindrance to physical healing.

There seems to have been an ongoing battle between the religious leaders of Judaism and the Lord Jesus Christ regarding His healing on the Sabbath Day. The healings brought Christ as much confrontation with the religious leaders as did His teachings. It seemed to delight Jesus to heal on the seventh day, for He saw this as a day to do good. He had come into the world to initiate a whole new dispensation and to bring about a grand day of deliverance and blessing and redemption.

Jesus did not hesitate to go against the stereotyped, traditional religious system that had laid hold of Judaism. He understood well that this was not the vital, live revelation that had come to God's ancient people, Israel, and that the Judaism of His day was a product of their own making.

Spiritual understanding

The healing ministry of the Lord Jesus in individuals

not only dealt with matters of personal sin, forgiveness, and the correction of a physical malady, but also resulted in an enlarged spiritual understanding. The blind man who was so graciously healed by the touch of the Lord Jesus was asked by the religious leaders to identify his healer.

> *The man answered and said to them, "Well, here is an amazing thing, that you do not know where He is from, and yet He opened my eyes. We know that God does not hear sinners; but if any one is God-fearing and does His will, He hears him. Since the beginning of time it has never been heard that any one opened the eyes of a person born blind. If this man were not from God, He could do nothing." They answered and said unto him, "You were born entirely in sins, and are you teaching us?" And they put him out.*
>
> *Jesus heard that they had put him out; and finding him, He said, "Do you believe in the Son of Man?" He answered and said, "And who is He, Lord, that I may believe in Him?" Jesus said to him, "You have both seen Him, and He is the one who is talking with you." And he said, "Lord, I believe." And he worshiped Him. And Jesus said, "For judgment I came into this world, that those who do not see may see; and that those who see may become blind"* (John 9:30-39).

Not only were the man's physical eyes opened, but the eyes of his heart were opened as well. Healing for him was a personal encounter with Christ, a realization of who Christ was. His healing led to adoration and worship.

The needy multitudes

In addition to the twenty-three individual miracles of

healing recorded in the Gospels, numerous multiple healings occurred as Christ ministered to great crowds of people. The following Scripture passages from the book of Matthew describe these mass healings:

> *And Jesus was going about in all Galilee, teaching in their synagogues, and proclaiming the gospel of the kingdom, and healing every kind of disease and every kind of sickness among the people. And the news about Him went out into all Syria; and they brought to Him all who were ill, taken with various diseases and pains, demoniacs, epileptics, paralytics; and He healed them* (4:23-24).
>
> *And Jesus was going about all the cities and the villages, teaching in their synagogues, and proclaiming the gospel of the kingdom, and healing every kind of disease and every kind of sickness* (9:35).
>
> *But Jesus, aware of this, withdrew from there. And many followed Him, and He healed them all* (12:15).
>
> *And when He came out, He saw a great multitude, and felt compassion for them, and healed their sick* (14:14).
>
> *And great multitudes came to Him, bringing with them those who were lame, crippled, blind, dumb, and many others, and they laid them down at His feet; and He healed them, so that the multitude marveled as they saw the dumb speaking, the crippled restored, and the lame walking, and the blind seeing; and they glorified the God of Israel* (15:30-31).

These passages demonstrate that Christ's mass healings were motivated by His concern for the needs of the crowd that stood before Him.

The signs and wonders in miraculous healings Jesus performed must not be seen as only demonstrations to validate His deity. To distort the simplicity of Christ's personality in order to accommodate preconceived doctrine may easily become a cultivated blindness. The signs and wonders were designed not only to awaken faith in the reality of who Jesus was but also to minister to needs that could be met in no other way. For Christ to have remained unmoved and coldly analytical in the face of the needs of multitudes who sought Him would have been entirely out of character for Him.

When the church of Jesus Christ experiences the true heart of Jesus by the Holy Spirit, marvelous workings in signs and wonders can be expected. But such experiences of blessing are not an end in themselves; rather, they are signs that lead ultimately toward redemption and disciplined discipleship—the cross, the resurrection, and body life in and through the church. Divine healing is the privilege of the believer; signs and wonders are but outbreakings to prepare the ground for the gospel and the whole counsel of God.

Frequently it is said that Christ "healed them all." There is no record that He ever rejected anyone who sought Him for physical healing during His earthly ministry. This is amazing! Was Jesus soft toward the needs of the multitudes He faced, and is He now removed from the mounting needs of far greater multitudes? Has He developed an unfeeling hardness? Hardly. Not if Hebrews 13:8 is believed. But Jesus Christ has committed His work to His church. It is for His followers to transmit the reality and compassion of Jesus.

The humanness of Christ

Christ was healer not only as God, but also as man. His

healing ministry was carried out in the power of the Holy
Spirit (Acts 10:38). His method reflects His humanity. He
responded to the touch of those who sought help.

> *And when they had come out of the boat, immediately
> the people recognized Him, and ran about that whole
> country and began to carry about on their pallets
> those who were sick, to the place they heard He was.
> And wherever He entered villages, or cities, or coun-
> tryside, they were laying the sick in the market places,
> and entreating Him that they might just touch the
> fringe of His cloak; and as many as touched it were
> being cured* (Mark 6:54-56).

> *And while the sun was setting, all who had any sick
> with various diseases brought them to Him; and lay-
> ing His hands on every one of them, He was healing
> them* (Luke 4:40).

There was winsomeness in the humanness of Jesus. Of
His childhood years we read: "And Jesus kept increasing
in wisdom and stature, and in favor with God and men"
(Luke 2:52). Jesus had a human life to live. The manifestation of true human existence in maturity was being revealed so human creatures made in His image might know
what they might aim at in life. Jesus was not giving tenta-
tive answers, He was giving final answers and divine healing was not excluded. He can be *touched* with the feelings
of our infirmities (Heb. 4:15).

It is of interest to read in Acts 2 that in the early church

> *many wonders and signs were taking place through
> the apostles. And all those who had believed were . . .
> continuing with one mind . . . , praising God, and
> having favor with all the people. And the Lord was*

adding to their number day by day those who were being saved (vv. 43-47).

There is a winsome humanness about Christlike people because their interest is in the needs of the multitudes outside the church. The tempo of our present day and the impersonalization about us desperately need an incursion of those who, like Christ, display a humanness that has compassion and understanding of need. Christ was rejected and crucified and the early church was experiencing the pressures of persecution, but human winsomeness came through sharp and clear.

Christ—a man filled with the Holy Spirit

Jesus healed both by the exercise of dynamic power and by the simple word of authority. Luke 5:17 says that the power of the Lord was present for Him to perform healing. This power was a dynamic, life-giving force that brought quickening to mortal bodies. Luke 7:20-21 reflects an important aspect of healing:

> *And when the men had come to Him, they said, "John the Baptist has sent us to You, saying, 'Are You the One who is coming, or do we look for someone else?' " At that very time He cured many people of diseases and afflictions and evil spirits; and He granted sight to many who were blind.*

On that particular occasion He manifested an authority, a right to grant healing as the Son of God.

The investigation by the messengers of John as to Jesus' identity was being answered by associating the works of Jesus with fulfillment of Old Testament prophecy concerning the Messiah (Isa. 35:4-5; 61:1 ff.). The aspect of promise and fulfillment was being substantiated by the sovereign Spirit of God in and through Jesus who had presented Himself to fulfill all righteousness and who was filled with the Holy Spirit (Matt. 3:13-17; Mark 3:7-11; Luke 3:21-22; 4:1; John 1:29-34).

Jesus Christ did not heal and perform miracles until that hour had arrived in His Father's will when He should begin His public ministry. His miracles were preceded by a mighty baptism of the Holy Spirit. It is most significant that Christ healed as a Spirit-filled man, a fact that strengthens the argument that it was His intention to confer this healing power upon His disciples and upon the church.

Further studies will demonstrate that during Christ's earthly ministry He conferred healing upon other men and that after His ascension to heaven He did the same thing.

Divine healing is not the performance of man for the glory of men, but the power of the Holy Spirit at work in those who are yielded and committed to the plan and purpose of God. Christ's exemplification was more than a performance, it was the human Jesus filled with the Holy Spirit ministering in obedience to the Father.

---

[1] Philip Vollmer, *Modern Students' Life of Christ*, p. 308.

[2] Henry B. Wilson, *Does Christ Still Heal?*, p. 49.

[3] Richard C. Trench, *Notes on the Miracles of Our Lord*, pp. 389-90.

7

The Healing Church

AS THE FOUR GOSPELS present the healing Christ, the Acts of the Apostles present the healing church. The church Christ is building in the world is the living expression of Himself. Through the instrumentality of the church Christ ministers today.

Luke said that the church described in the book of Acts was a continuation of that which Jesus taught and did. The book suggests no termination point for this work. The New Testament Epistles also infer that the church persists in the work to the close of this age.

In the light of these facts, it is reasonable to assume that the work of ministry in the apostolic church was determinative for the church in the future. The church ministers not merely on principles or on tradition but by the very life and will of the crowned Christ. The healing ministry of the early church gives evidence of this truth. Christ was still healing, but through the church.

Christ conferred the ministry of healing
upon the church

The church is not presuming when she carries out the ministry of healing. Three passages of Scripture will serve to demonstrate that the power of healing can be conferred upon men by Christ and that it was His intention that such authority to heal should continue in the church.

> *And He called the twelve together, and gave them power and authority over all the demons, and to heal diseases* (Luke 9:1).

> *Now after this the Lord appointed seventy others and sent them two and two ahead of Him to every city and place where He Himself was going to come. And He was saying to them, ". . . And whatever city you enter, and they receive you, eat what is set before you; and heal those in it who are sick"* (10:1-2a, 8-9a).

> *"And these signs will accompany those who have believed: in My name they will cast out demons, they will speak with new tongues; they will pick up serpents, and if they drink any deadly poison, it shall not hurt them; they will lay hands on the sick, and they will recover"* (Mark 16:17-18).

The early Christians did not have a preoccupation with physical healing. But as they served and boldly proclaimed Christ in all His fullness the blessing of healing was evident. Their interest was focused on the Lord Jesus Christ. He was always central. To the believers of that day, that Christ should heal seemed most obvious.

The Acts

The healings mentioned in Acts offer important detail

that deserves careful study. Healings most frequently occurred in the wake of great spiritual revival.

Both healing and exorcism in the book of Acts occurred in the evangelistic situation. Michael Green has captured this truth in his book, *Evangelism in the Early Church.*

> Christians went out into the world as exorcizers and healers as well as preachers. The Acts is full of "signs and wonders" of exorcism and healing which backed up the Christian claim that Jesus had conquered the demonic forces on the cross, that He had come to bring salvation or health to the whole man, not merely his soul.[1]

The effectiveness of apostolic evangelism can be at least partly attributed to the attendant ministry of healing.

The lame man at the temple gate

The first miracle of the apostolic age was a physical healing. Peter and John, on their way to the temple for prayer, encountered a crippled beggar. Suddenly Peter was moved by the Holy Spirit to say to the man now looking to them for a donation of money:

> *"I do not possess silver and gold, but what I do have I give to you: In the name of Jesus Christ the Nazarene —walk!"* (Acts 3:6)

Peter then extended his hand to the startled man and began to lift him. At that instance faith released the mighty power of the living Christ and that poor beggar leaped to his feet. With uncontrollable joy he ran and walked and leaped. The Scripture records that along with the physical manifestation of his healing the man also began to praise God.

The healing of the lame man took place at the Beautiful Gate, the east gate to the temple area. It was a busy concourse, especially at the time of day when the miracle occurred. The beggar was no stranger to the people who came regularly to the temple to pray.

The immediate effect of the lame man's healing was electrifying. People literally ran from every direction to see this happy man running and leaping in his newfound strength.

The apostle took immediate advantage of the situation and began to preach to the assembled crowd. His first concern was to establish the fact that neither he nor John had healed the lame man; the risen and glorified Son of God, Jesus Christ, had healed him. Peter proceeded to preach Christ to them, and his sermon is a masterpiece of evangelistic persuasion. It also contains some gems of truth about divine healing.

> *"And on the basis of faith in His name, it is the name of Jesus which has strengthened this man whom you see and know; and the faith which comes through Him has given him this perfect health in the presence of you all"* (v. 16).

The lame man had been healed through faith in the name of Jesus. The divine name is representative of all the powers, grace, gifts, and benefits Christ is pleased to bestow on men. His name is descriptive of His very nature, Christ the Healer.

Mass healings in the book of Acts

The book of Acts records several incidents in which mass healings took place. These incidents, in their proper context, give valuable insight into the purpose and providence of God.

After the healing of the lame man and Peter's message

on the power and authority of the risen Christ, a great number of people believed, and the rulers who had crucified Christ became alarmed at the spreading report of Christ's resurrection and the growing popularity of Christians.

Consequently, Peter and John were arrested. After one night in prison (4:5, 21) they were brought before the Sanhedrin and questioned: "By what power, or in what name, have you done this?" (v. 7).

Then Peter, with John and the man healed of lameness standing beside him, exalting the Christ who had been crucified, proclaimed the salvation message. The council was stunned both because of the living testimony of the man who had been lame and because of the boldness of the apostles.

Peter and John were threatened and commanded not to teach in the name of Jesus, but they said,

> *"Whether it is right in the sight of God to give heed to you rather than to God, you be the judge; for we cannot stop speaking what we have seen and heard"* (vv. 19-20).

Finally, after further threats, they were released. Immediately they joined the Jerusalem assembly in a prayer meeting and reported what had been said. The assembly, in oneness, lifted their voices to God in exaltation of Christ:

> *"And now, Lord, take note of their threats, and grant that Thy bond-servants may speak Thy word with all confidence, While Thou dost extend Thy hand to heal, and signs and wonders take place through the name of Thy holy Servant Jesus"* (vv. 29-30).

Having recognized the results that had followed the

healing of the lame man, the early Christians asked for healings as signs and wonders, and with the petition the church committed herself to a bold witness regardless of the cost.

Chapter five reveals the exposure of Ananias and his wife for their hypocrisy and their judgment by the hand of God. A wave of fear of the Lord swept over the church and apparently over the community. Large numbers of people turned to Christ as a result of this manifestation; in the wake of the revival, physical healing occurred on a large scale.

> *And all the more believers in the Lord, multitudes of men and women, were constantly added to their number; to such an extent that they even carried the sick out into the streets, and laid them on cots and pallets, so that when Peter came by, at least his shadow might fall on any one of them. And also the people from the cities in the vicinity of Jerusalem were coming together, bringing people who were sick or afflicted with unclean spirits; and they were all being healed* (vv. 14-16).

At least two other similar movements of mass healings are recorded in Acts. When the persecution broke out in Jerusalem, Philip the deacon was forced to flee to Samaria. He began preaching the gospel with remarkable results. Many sought the Lord and were baptized as a result of the ministry of Philip. Acts 8:7 describes the mass healings which attended Philip's meetings.

> *For in the case of many who had unclean spirits, they were coming out of them shouting with a loud voice; and many who had been paralyzed and lame were healed.*

These attesting miracles had a great effect upon the community of unconverted people. Luke points out that the miracles were a major factor in turning many to Christ (v. 6).

The apostle Paul also witnessed incidents of mass healing in his missionary activities. The most striking of them took place in the city of Ephesus. The renewal of small bands of disciples there resulted in a citywide revival. The predominant feature of this revival was evangelism. For two years the church in Ephesus spread out over the province of Asia in what is perhaps the greatest incident of concentrated evangelism in the history of the church.

The revival at Ephesus was not a healing campaign, but the ministry of healing was an important feature of the revival. Luke records the healing phenomena.

> *And God was performing extraordinary miracles by the hands of Paul, so that handkerchiefs or aprons were even carried from his body to the sick, and the diseases left them and the evil spirits went out* (19:11-12).

The mass healings took place not because certain men noted for "the gift of healing" had risen to prominence by conducting healing campaigns, but they took place when the church experienced divine quickening and evangelism took on a bold strategy of offense in confrontation with the world in need.

Aeneas

Chapter nine of Acts records another healing in which Peter was the human instrument.

> *Now it came about that as Peter was traveling through all those parts, he came down also to the saints who lived at Lydda. And there he found a certain man*

named Aeneas, who had been bedridden eight years,
for he was paralyzed. And Peter said to him, "Aeneas,
Jesus Christ heals you; arise, and make your bed."
And immediately he arose. And all who lived at Lydda
and Sharon saw him, and they turned to the Lord
(vv. 32-35).

This passage, even more clearly than chapter three, presents Christ in His office of healer. Peter told Aeneas, "Jesus Christ heals you." The Lord Jesus Christ is Healer in His name and in His nature and in His position. Healing is forever His prerogative.

The methodology of healing ministry practiced by the early church always made clear to seekers and observers that healing came through Christ and Him alone. When excited crowds attempted to give the apostles a healer image they publicly renounced it and gave Christ the glory. Christ's church on earth is just the yielded instrument through which Christ now heals from His position on high.

Variety in the healing events

The book of Acts contains twenty references to divine healings ministered by the early Christians. The methods used are varied. The ministry of healing was not restricted to apostles. Laymen like Stephen, Philip, and Ananias were used of the Lord to heal physical afflictions.

Anointing with oil is not mentioned in the Acts. The laying on of hands is mentioned twice. Some healings occurred by the command of faith; others, by prayer, by touch, or by tokens such as handkerchiefs. A more developed procedure for the ministry of healing came with the completion of the New Testament Scriptures.

The last record of healing in the Acts of the Apostles is

in chapter twenty-eight. Paul was shipwrecked on an island inhabited by pagans. It was raining when Paul and his companions came ashore. As they gathered wood for a fire, a poisonous viper bit Paul. The natives watched, expecting him to drop dead. When Paul showed no ill effects from the bite, this miracle made a deep impression on them.

Paul then learned that the father of the ruler of the island was seriously ill.

> *And it came about that the father of Publius was lying in bed afflicted with recurrent fever and dysentery; and Paul went in to see him and after he had prayed, he laid his hands on him and healed him. And after this had happened, the rest of the people on the island who had diseases were coming to him and getting cured* (vv. 8-9).

This account is a pure example of "signs following" according to Mark 16:17. The healings on this island of Melita were sovereign acts of God worked through the apostle.

Note that the text says that Paul laid his hands on him and healed him. This is the strongest statement in the Bible with regard to the human instrument in the ministry of healing. The Scripture records that Paul prayed prior to laying on hands so the pagan would know in whose name he healed.

Nothing is said of the spiritual effects on those healed by Paul. But it must be assumed that many who enjoyed the healing touch of Christ turned to Him as their Savior. Church history tells of a church on this island from a very early date. The healing signs are for the sake of confirming the gospel where it has never been preached.

The New Testament Epistles

The critics of the church's ministry of healing have objected to its continuation on the ground that the Epistles are silent on the subject. But if one scans the New Testament Epistles, he can find no less than ten passages on the matter of healing.

The Epistles deal with the doctrine of healing in a manner distinctly different from the historical portions of the New Testament. Healing is not treated in isolation but always in relationship to other theological concepts.

Romans

The first reference to physical healing in the Epistles is Romans 8:11.

> *But if the Spirit of Him who raised Jesus from the dead dwells in you, He who raised Christ Jesus from the dead will also give life to your mortal bodies through His Spirit who indwells you.*

Paul teaches the possibility of a life-giving touch from God in our present physical bodies. The "mortal" body refers to a living body. Unfortunately, many scholars have interpreted Paul's statement as a prediction of the resurrection of the Christian's body. It is true that Paul teaches such a doctrine, but the modifier used in this verse points to a divine quickening of living Christians and not dead Christians.

The word *mortal* is used five times in the New Testament. The basic idea of the Greek word translated "mortal" is dying or subject to death. The usage in 6:12 is helpful: *Therefore do not let sin reign in your mortal body.* No one would question the fact that Paul is addressing a living person in this passage.

Another usage occurs in Second Corinthians 4:11: *that the life of Jesus also may be manifested in our mortal flesh.* The condition in the context makes clear that the apostle speaks of the manifestation of the death and life of Christ in the bodies of living persons.

The other two occurrences of the word *mortal* are in the great resurrection chapter, First Corinthians 15.

> *For this perishable must put on the imperishable, and this mortal must put on immortality. But when this perishable will have put on the imperishable, and this mortal will have put on immortality, then will come about the saying that is written,* "DEATH IS SWALLOWED UP IN VICTORY" (vv. 53-54).

This passage speaks of the rapture of living saints. Paul explains to the Corinthians that not all Christians will die physically. When Christ comes for His own, the living will be translated without dying. At that moment they will exchange their mortal condition for the blessed state of immortality.

All five usages of *mortal* in Paul's writings refer to living believers.

Paul taught that believers could experience a quickening of their bodies through the indwelling Holy Spirit. The quickening by the Spirit appears to be a firstfruit of the resurrection. The emphasis of Romans 8:11 is the similarity of the quickening and the resurrection. When the child of God is quickened physically through the Holy Spirit he is receiving a foretaste of the resurrection. Paul addresses this concept of physical quickening to the church. He is speaking of healing as the privilege of the believer.

Charles Spurgeon preached a sermon on June 11, 1882, entitled "Jehovah-Rapha." It was based on the text in

Exodus 15:26. Spurgeon sets forth Christ as the Healer of our circumstances, our bodies, and our souls. That section of his sermon on the healing of the body ought to be read by all who are serious about the Lord's provision for healing. Spurgeon expresses the idea that bodily healing foretells bodily resurrection.

> Note this, that in every healing of which we are the subjects we have a pledge of the resurrection. Every time a man who is near the gates of death rises up again he enjoys a kind of rehearsal of the grand rising when from beds of dust and silent clay the perfect saints shall rise at the trump of the archangel and the voice of God. We ought to gather from our restorations from serious and perilous sickness a proof that the God who brings us back from the gates of the grave can also bring us back from the grave itself whenever it shall be time to do so.[2]

First and Second Corinthians

The two letters of Paul addressed to the church at Corinth help round out the Pauline concept of life for the body. The Corinthians had a problem with the sins of the body. Their culture had become so degenerate that sensuality was accepted as a way of life. Many of the Christians were having a real struggle with the temptation associated with the sensual. Paul pointed them to the revelation of God regarding the sanctity of the Christian's body.

In the midst of his discussion, Paul makes a summary statement on the relationship of the body to the Lord.

> *Food is for the stomach, and the stomach is for food; but God will do away with both of them. Yet the body is not for immorality, but for the Lord; and the Lord is for the body* (1 Cor. 6:13).

This verse presents the principle that the believer has the responsibility to dedicate wholly his body to the Lord.

The biblical doctrine of health and healing always has spiritual implications. God does not accommodate self-willed men with healing benefit just because He is God and has power to heal. The normal doctrine of healing calls for the total consecration of the body to Christ. Again the Scriptures emphasize healing as the privilege of the redeemed.

The divine response to the believer's consecration is the remarkable provision of the Lord for the body. In its broadest sense this statement has reference to everything Christ provides for the physical body, not just healing. The Lord for the body means salvation, sanctification, glorification, and healing as a part of a total redemption. Such a perspective of healing will keep the truth rightly related to the whole.

But something more than healing is inherent in the Lord for the body. The Christian whose body is weak from a medical standpoint may experience the Lord for the body with little, if any, change in the physical condition. Christ so quickens the body that he has strength to carry out his work while his physical condition should make him an invalid. The indwelling Christ manifests his life in the whole man, giving that person a wholesome mental attitude and strength to function for the glory of God.

It is possible also for a Christian with a sound physical body to enjoy the benefits of the Lord for the body. One does not have to be sick to derive physical good from the provision of Christ for the body, for Christ is the giver of health as well as of healing. A constant state of physical well-being is more desirable than a miracle of healing. The indwelling Christ manifests His life to the spirit, soul, and body of the believer. A constant and unbroken union of the believer with the risen Christ means a flow of His very life ministering well-being to the whole person.

The supernatural strengthening of the body is an ancient truth. The Old Testament Scriptures offer several examples of believers whose bodies were quickened by the Spirit of God. Such quickening was given to enable that saint to accomplish the divine purpose in his life.

Moses knew such a manifestation of life for the body. Joshua, Caleb, and Samson—all experienced Spirit-imparted physical strength. These examples establish the fact that God, by His Holy Spirit, quickens the physical body with great vitality and strength.

The Holy Spirit taught Paul a doctrine of divine life for the body more developed than in the Old Testament. Paul explains to the Corinthians that holding such an exalted view of the body, one could appropriate life from Christ for that body. The death and the life of the Lord Jesus Christ are to be manifested in the personality of the Christian. There is much benefit in beginning each day with a reminder of this wonderful aspect of one's relationship to Christ.

The physical heritage of the believer through Christ includes the healing of disease, the promotion of health, and protection from disease. It is difficult to believe and take in all that God has provided. Many believers have considered the doctrine of healing only when they have reached a crisis of serious sickness.

The teaching of Paul is so broad that every believer every day can appropriate its blessing. Whether in sickness or in good health the body is for the Lord and the Lord is for the body. Regardless of the believer's condition from the medical viewpoint, he may claim an exhibition of the life of Jesus Christ in his mortal flesh (2 Cor. 4:11).

Could anything bring a greater sense of the sacredness of life than this concept? Does it not call for a careful and a holy walk? Such a doctrine of divine healing is not a preoccupation with one's physical illnesses and a morbid effort by any and all means to be delivered from them, but rather a high level of union with Christ resulting in the whole personality becoming an instrument for the manifestation of the living Christ.

Among the Pauline passages related to the doctrine of healing is First Corinthians 11:23-32:

> *For I received from the Lord that which I also delivered to you, that the Lord Jesus in the night in which He was betrayed took bread; and when He had given thanks, He broke it, and said, "This is My body, which is for you; do this in remembrance of Me." In the same way the cup also, after supper, saying, "This cup is the new covenant in My blood; do this, as often as you drink it, in remembrance of Me." For as often as you eat this bread and drink the cup, you proclaim the Lord's death until He comes. Therefore whoever eats the bread or drinks the cup of the Lord in an unworthy manner, shall be guilty of the body and the blood of the Lord. But let a man examine himself, and so let him eat of the bread and drink of the cup. For he who eats and drinks, eats and drinks judgment to himself, if he does not judge the body rightly. For this reason many among you are weak and sick, and a number sleep. But if we judged ourselves rightly, we should not be judged. But when we are judged, we are disciplined by the Lord in order that we may not be condemned along with the world.*

Without engaging in a full doctrinal treatment of the ordinance of communion, the meaning of verses 29 and 30 should be carefully explored. Paul quite boldly remarks that a number of people within the Corinthian assembly were physically weak or invalids as a result of an improper taking of communion. Some of the members had actually died from physical ailments inflicted as direct judgment from God on their unworthy approach to the Lord's table. It has already been established that sickness sometimes comes to believers as chastisement from the Lord. Careless believers who came unprepared to the communion opened themselves to such chastening.

A key to this passage is the phrase in verse 29: *if he does not judge the body rightly.*

Commentators fall into two camps in their interpretation of "the body." Some believe that it has reference to the church as the body of Christ; others, to the actual body and blood of Christ. That one interpretation is exclusive of the other is highly improbable. Note the context which precedes the oft-quoted passage just observed:

> *But in giving this instruction, I do not praise you, because you come together not for the better but for the worse. For, in the first place, when you come together as a church, I hear that divisions exist among you; and in part, I believe it. For there must also be factions among you, in order that those who are approved may have become evident among you. Therefore when you meet together, it is not to eat the Lord's Supper, for in your eating each one takes his own supper first; and one is hungry and another is drunk* (vv. 17-20).

The night that Jesus instituted the Supper He taught the disciples a lesson in humility by washing their feet; the symbolism of its meaning is recorded in John 13:1-17. Examination of one's spiritual walk was necessary before the Supper was to be observed. The disciples had argued among themselves as to their individual rank in relationship to Jesus; most likely the neglect of their etiquette was a result of the attitudes and feelings that had arisen. John records:

> *Jesus, knowing that the Father had given all things into His hands, and that He had come forth from God, and was going back to God, rose from supper, and laid aside His garments; and taking a towel, girded Himself about* (vv. 3-4).

Factions and divisions at the table of the Lord are a deliberate neglect and an offense to the significance of the Lord's body as referring both to the person of Christ and to His church. Jesus instructed the disciples:

> *"If I then, the Lord and the Teacher, washed your feet, you also ought to wash one another's feet. For I gave you an example that you also should do as I did to you"* (vv. 14-15).

The worshiper, however, is to discern or judge the body of Christ and the sacrifice Christ has made. When the Christian takes the Lord's Supper with an unprepared heart and an indifferent attitude he eats and drinks judgment. The three conditions mentioned in First Corinthians 11:30 do not exhaust the chastenings a sovereign God may determine. Apparently, physical ailments are often the form of judgment God uses. The association of man's physical and spiritual natures cannot be overlooked. The correction of the spiritual condition in these cases is a pathway to healing; the vertical relationship to God has a horizontal association with the brethren.

A positive meaning may also be given Paul's phrase *discerning the body*. If failure to discern brings chastening, then the faithfulness of thoughtful discernments should bring blessing. The Lord's table is a place of worship, thanksgiving, praise, reconciliation, and even learning.

No one can meditate long upon the dying form of Jesus without learning something new and precious about the mercy and forgiveness of God and how this should be reflected among believers. Gathering at the Lord's table is an appropriate time for believers to examine their relationships and exercise their faith. Having comprehended the benefits of the sacrifice of Christ, how natural to appropriate them by faith.

A. B. Simpson wrote:

> Here He promises us not only spiritual life, but physical life from His own body. This is the blessed truth which our faith has learned to apprehend in the Lord's Supper. It is the truth commonly known as divine healing. It is deeper than mere healing, and it is the actual participation in the physical strength, vitality and energy of our risen Lord.[3]

Dr. Simpson was not alone in understanding healing as one of the blessings of the Lord's table. The Book of Common Prayer of the Anglican Church contains promises and prayers for the recovery of health as well as for the correction of the believer's spiritual condition.

Philippians

The details of one healing can be found in the New Testament Epistles. Paul's fellow worker, Epaphroditus, hovered between life and death. From Paul's statement regarding him it appears that he became exhausted from overwork. Epaphroditus came from Philippi, where he was the director of the church, to minister to Paul during his imprisonment.

Paul records with openness and honesty his reaction to Epaphroditus's sickness. He was greatly concerned for his friend and at times held little hope for his recovery. The believers at Philippi also were greatly exercised about him.

These reactions indicate that Paul and his fellow workers did not hold a view of "push-button" healing in which one could pray anytime and get immediate results.

The viewpoint held by some scholars that Paul had by this time lost his power to heal has no basis. The delay and difficulty in healing in this case were a matter of divine sovereignty. The believers accepted it as such.

Most commentators overlook the fact that the recovery of Epaphroditus was an incident of divine healing because he was not healed instantly and miraculously. Paul says that Epaphroditus recovered from his serious illness by means of divine intervention: *God had mercy on him* (Phil. 2:27).

The case of Epaphroditus is one among many which show that divine healing is not always instantaneous. Many believers become discouraged if they do not experience immediate results after prayer and anointing. Persistence in faith is necessary. Delays in healing are often related to spiritual issues with which God is pleased to deal before granting recovery.

First Timothy

Paul's concept of healing included what A. T. Pierson has called "the holy care of the body." The Christian is called upon to glorify God in his body. The weird notions regarding the body prevalent in the monasticism of the Middle Ages have no ground in Scripture.

Paul saw the body as an earthly vessel with a heavenly treasure in it. The body, then, deserves the care it needs to glorify God. Paul was very practical at this point. The Holy Spirit saw to it that the Word of God preserved Paul's advice to a fellow worker with regard to the sensible care of his body.

> *No longer drink water exclusively, but use a little wine for the sake of your stomach and your frequent ailments* (5:23).

Young Timothy apparently suffered frequent attacks of sickness. In Paul's judgment, the simple practice of avoiding water, which was probably contaminated, and the use of wine in its place would improve Timothy's health. Proper diet, adequate sleep, exercise, and cleanliness are as much a part of the Bible doctrine of divine healing as is anointing and prayer. Christians have an obligation to give proper care to their bodies.

Third John

Perhaps the most philosophic statement on healing in the Epistles is in the third letter of the apostle John.

> *Beloved, I pray that in all respects you may prosper and be in good health, just as your soul prospers* (v. 2).

The relationship of the body to the soul is central in this passage. John was expressing his prayerful concern for Gaius, his brother in Christ, that he might enjoy a general state of prosperity.

It is generally true that prosperity of soul and prosperity of body go together. But it is not correct to reason that this is always so regardless of the circumstances. Some of the most precious saints alive today suffer from physical affliction. These cases are exceptions, not the rule. Generally, soul blessing is an aid to good health. Both the Old and New Testament Scriptures teach this truth.

James

The key Scripture passage regarding the continued practice of the ministry of healing throughout the church age is James 5:13-18. These divinely inspired instructions have never been revoked. Some rather strange rules of interpretation have been devised in an effort to avoid the obvious meaning of these verses. But the practice of anointing has persisted from apostolic days until now.

What James was constrained to write on the doctrine provides insight as to its practice and some basic truths as to the theology of healing. The apostle emphasizes the relationship of healing and prayer. In these six verses seven references are made to prayer. The Lord Jesus taught James that the right kind of praying is the essential climate for the church's ministry of healing.

The believer must pray for himself when faced with physical need. The elders have a special responsibility to pray the prayers of faith when anointing. The whole assembly is called upon to pray for one another when some member of the assembly suffers from a physical malady. The pattern of prayer for healing, according to the Scripture, is a ministry shared by the whole church.

Someone may protest that such a concerted program of prayer for healing places too much emphasis on the physical need. A closer look at the passage will prove just the opposite to be true. Prayer is a spiritual exercise. Praying on this level described by James touches a number of spiritual issues. Such concentrated praying keeps the healing ministry in perspective. Prayer helps to uncover the underlying spiritual needs of the individual seeking healing. His heart is made aware of his total need. The church is challenged by prayer and is called upon to cleanse herself. From the positive side, the church is moved to exercise faith.

James's words on the anointing procedure imply that the spiritual exercise required takes some time and careful consideration. The effectiveness of the church's healing ministry depends upon how seriously this passage is taken by everyone involved—the candidate for anointing, the elders, and the whole assembly. If this full spectrum of prayer for healing were carried out, the number of incidents of divine healing would be greatly increased. Much failure in the use of anointing comes from a hurried partial carrying out of the scriptural practice.

Instructions for the individual who is sick are very explicit. He should first of all call for the elders of the church. *Church* here means the local church. The issue of obedience is at stake. There is little hope of exercising any kind of real faith if obedience is absent from the heart. However we may feel about the practice of anointing, it is God's method. The whole concept came by revelation. The instruction to call for the elders in the event of sickness is a part of the Word of God and cannot be ignored by any serious believer.

To summon the elders calls the Christian's attention to the fact that he is dependent and needs God's help in everything. His physical, as well as spiritual, problems have their ultimate answer in the finished work of Christ. To call for the elders is a humble admission of need. What better heart attitude than this for receiving the blessing of the Lord! The personal preparation for anointing, according to James, requires deep heart searching. The sufferer must not only relate his physical need to the spiritual but also search his heart for any sin that could stand as a barrier to God's healing touch. The sin should be confessed and put under the blood of Christ.

Everything about this passage seems designed to cultivate faith. The apostle was not suggesting that on rare or unusual occasions one might hope that anointing would result in healing, but he asserts a positive expectation that anointing will result in healing. The exceptions are not under discussion here. Those who are actually looking to God for healing are encouraged to call for the elders of the church.

To carry out a hollow, meaningless ceremony of anointing void of any faith for healing violates the whole spirit of James's message to the church. The ceremony in itself has no virtue and imparts no blessing. The design of the unction is to draw attention to spiritual truth. God Himself is the only Healer. The anointing oil symbolizes the direct and immediate work of the Holy Spirit. The Spirit, not the oil, gives life to the body.

The instructions speak of elders rather than one elder. There is significance to a plurality of elders. When a group of elders pray, no one knows which of the elders actually prayed the prayer of faith for healing. The human agent is kept in the background. God alone receives the glory.

The consistent observance of this instruction will safeguard the integrity of the church's healing ministry. No one gets a reputation as a healer. This is the error of many healing movements today.

It should be further observed that the ministry of healing taught in the New Testament is always in an assembly context. It is a local-church affair. Extracurricular meetings find no authorization in the Scriptures. Healing sign-miracles did occur during revivals and evangelistic meetings recorded in the book of Acts. But these were not meetings called for healing. Healing occurred incidentally on these occasions.

The only authorized healing service for the church is James 5:13-18. It is a church meeting, not a public affair. It is for believers. Since it affects one member of the body of Christ, all other members of the body are affected.

The church's involvement in the healing of a sick member is not complete with the anointing and prayer of the elders. Verse 16 says:

> *Therefore, confess your sins to one another, and pray for one another, so that you may be healed. The effective prayer of a righteous man can accomplish much.*

The whole assembly comes in view. The members of the body minister to one another. Not only the sick member and the elders but all the members carry out this injunction.

Confession is the heart preparation for prayer. The mood of prayer under these circumstances is not that of panic. It is not a mood of demands that God heal. The original language suggests rather that the prayers of the church now cleansed and spiritually renewed are prayers of worship and adoration. The purpose of the prayer meeting, then, is not to persuade God to heal but to prepare the hearts of the saints to receive the blessing of healing.

The prayers of the elders reflect this same mood of loving worship to God in Christ's name. They first pray over the sick person. Such prayer prepares both the heart of the one suffering affliction and the hearts of the ministering elders for what is to follow. The sick should then be anointed "in the name of the Lord."

Since the text does not say "the Lord Jesus Christ," it can be implied that the whole Trinity is involved when the sick are anointed. For all three persons of the Godhead are addressed by this very high term for Deity. *Lord* in the New Testament is the equivalent of *Jehovah* in the Old Testament. This name speaks of God as the Eternal and All-Sufficient One. It seems from this passage that it is appropriate to anoint the sick in the name of the Father and of the Son and of the Holy Spirit.

Anointing in His name forever establishes this fact that God alone is the Healer. James further sustains this truth by saying, "And the Lord will raise him up" (v. 15). The instruments of anointing and prayer are only incidental in the divine act of bodily healing.

Verse 16 says:

> *The effective prayer of a righteous man can accomplish much.*

The emphasis in the verse is lost in most English translations. Herman Hoyt translates the verse in these words:

> *The prayer of a righteous man, which is energized (wrought) in him accomplishes much.* [4]

It is true that righteous men pray effectively, but James is saying also that the kind of praying needed on this occasion finds its inspiration in God Himself. The Holy Spirit energizes the believer for such powerful praying. No doubt the prayer of faith is a prayer resulting from the special energizing of the Holy Spirit.

There is much about the order of ministry to the sick which calls attention to the work of the Holy Spirit in healing. The anointing oil symbolizes the Holy Spirit. The spiritual preparation of the sick for anointing and the spiritual preparation of the church for anointing require an in-depth working of the Holy Spirit. The Holy Spirit is always the immediate agent of the blessing of redemption through Christ. The healing virtue of the crowned Christ is administered to the body of the believer by the Holy Spirit.

The practice of laying on hands at the time of anointing gives further emphasis to the work of the Spirit. The laying on of hands in the New Testament is most frequently associated with prayer for the fullness of the Holy Spirit, but it is also clearly associated with prayer for the sick, as the following verses illustrate:

And He could do no miracle there except that He laid His hands upon a few sick people and healed them (Mark 6:5).

And these signs will accompany those who have believed: in My name they will cast out demons, they will speak with new tongues; they will pick up serpents, and if they drink any deadly poison, it shall not hurt them; they will lay hands on the sick, and they will recover (16:17-18).

And it came about that the father of Publius was lying in bed afflicted with recurrent fever and dysentery; and Paul went in to see him and after he had prayed, he laid his hands on him and healed him (Acts 28:8).

Like anointing, the laying on of hands symbolizes spiritual reality. It speaks of the communication of divine blessing through the ministry of the Holy Spirit.

The anointing with oil has sometimes been interpreted as medical therapy rather than ecclesiastical unction. If such were the case, it would introduce an element completely foreign to the context. Everything about the passage points to a spiritual ministry. The nursing care of the sick is not under discussion here. That the elders of the church should perform this nurse-care function is unrealistic. The elders anointing with oil in the name of the Lord for healing by means of divine intervention, is the teaching of this passage.

The ecclesiastical view of anointing is further sustained by the statement in Mark 6:13:

And they were casting out many demons and were anointing with oil many sick people and healing them.

The use of oil by the apostles resulted in instantaneous

healings. Oil, as a medical treatment, does not produce immediate healing. The apostles no doubt used anointing with oil to encourage faith in those seeking healing. Those scholars who contend for a medical use of oil in James 5 admit that the usage in Mark 6:13 cannot be medical. The same Greek verb is used in both passages. It is reasonable to conclude that the anointing has a symbolic meaning in both passages and is associated with healing through quickening of the Holy Spirit.

The Scripture mentions no effect of anointing in Mark 6:13 other than immediate bodily healing. James, expanding the doctrine, shows that anointing during the church age is for believers and will result not only in physical healing but in spiritual healing as well, when such is needed. However, when James adds, "And if he has committed sins, they shall be forgiven him," the implication is not that forgiveness of sin will be a mere fringe benefit, for James gives further explanation in what immediately follows:

> *Therefore, confess your sins to one another, and pray for one another, so that you may be healed. The effective prayer of a righteous man can accomplish much* (v. 16).

Effective praying is holy praying, and healing will be coincident with right praying. But the deeper implication is that faith is not to be hindered by morbid introspection that equates faith and healing with personal righteousness. There is ground for anointing with oil and praying for the sick even though the imperfection of unconscious short-comings are with us.

Healing, holiness, and prayer are closely associated in the believer because the whole man and the whole person-ality are in the purview of divine purpose and the atonement avails for both. Christ works from within outward, beginning with the spiritual nature and then diffusing His life and power through the physical being.

What is the appropriate time and place for a service of anointing? Some hold rigidly to the position that since the sick call for the elders, the anointing service should be in the privacy of their home or hospital room. Certainly for those patients who are incapacitated, the home or hospital is the place to conduct the anointing service. But it should be understood that the church gathering is also a proper place to anoint the sick. Many seriously ill people are able and prefer to attend the regular services of the church.

Another aspect of this question is the involvement of the whole assembly in the ministry of healing as discussed earlier. If the assembly is to engage in mutual prayer and heart searching, then it seems that the service of anointing would be greatly enriched if conducted in such an atmosphere. If the healing service never occurs in the assembly, it would be difficult to enlist the involvement of the whole church in this ministry.

Since the members of the body are to minister to one another, the church gathering is the place for such a ministry. The undergirding of mutual love, faith, and understanding is of infinite value to the suffering member of the body seeking healing. The confession prayer, or testimony of a brother or sister in Christ, may well spark the fire of faith in a depressed mind of the sick person.

Regular services of healing observing the order of James 5 will strengthen the spiritual tone of any church. It will open up avenues of outreach to needy people in the community. Such a practice is a beautiful demonstration of New Testament body life resulting in the growth of all members of the fellowship.

[1]Michael Green, *Evangelism in the Early Church,* p. 189.

[2]C. H. Spurgeon, *The Metropolitan Pulpit,* Vol. 28, p. 332.

[3]A. B. Simpson, *First Corinthians: The Principles and Life of the Apostolic Church,* pp. 89-90.

[4]Herman A. Hoyt, *All Things Whatsoever I Have Commanded You,* p. 48.

8

The Gifts of Healings

WHILE THE GIFTS OF the Holy Spirit existed and operated in Old Testament times, they came into full view during New Testament days.

The revival movements within the church since the Reformation have varied in their emphasis on the work and gifts of the Spirit. But a number of these movements, as the chapter on the historical development of the doctrine of healing will verify, saw a renewal of the gifts of healing.

The need for biblical understanding

During the twentieth century the emerging Pentecostal movement has placed a strong emphasis on the charisma of healing. The contemporary Charismatic movement holds a similar viewpoint. The result in many instances has been the emerging of the "healer" concept. A pastor or an evangelist who has particular success praying for the sick is then looked upon by the church as having the gift of healing. He becomes a specialist in healing. The unfortunate outcome of such a practice is that man rather than Christ receives glory when results do occur.

The major Scripture passages dealing with the gifts are First Corinthians 12 and 14, Romans 12:3-8, and Ephesians 4:7-16. But only in First Corinthians 12 do we find "gifts of healing" (vv. 9, 28, 30). The theme of the chapter is the unity in which the "one and the same Spirit" (v. 11) distributes and administers the varieties of gifts within the one body of Christ at Corinth.

The reader should peruse First Corinthians 12, 13, and 14 a number of times to fix in his mind the context into which the gifts are introduced. The Corinthian epistle is the best cross-section of early church life the Holy Spirit has preserved for us. The body of Christ, the church, is central in this whole passage. All the gifts must be studied in the context of the body life of the church.

Particular gifts—such as apostles, prophets, evangelists, and pastor-teachers (1 Cor. 12:28; see Rom. 12:6-8; Eph. 4:11-16)—have *modi operandi* and serve as regular support for the ministry of the church as a whole and equip the church for ministering. The majority of the gifts mentioned are for mutual edification and strength and are representative of the entire church.

"Gifts of healings" were associated with certain members in the church at Corinth (1 Cor. 12:30), but these members were not known as "divine healers." "Gifts of healings" were spontaneous within the assembly; their exercise implied the rendering of service among believers.

The charismatic gifts are designed primarily for ministry to the body of Christ, the church. Gifts presented with an individualistic approach will most likely become perverted. This has been true especially of the gifts of healings.

The significance of the plural

An important feature of the healing charisma is that it occurs in the plural—*gifts* of healings. It is evident from this construction that the Holy Spirit has distributed supernatural endowments or gifts of power for the physical restoration of the sick—particularly "effecting of miracles" (1 Cor. 12:9-10, 28, 29-30) and "gifts of healings," both of which appear in the plural. In the book of Acts, miracles *(dynameis)* were associated with bodily healing and the casting out of evil spirits (8:6-7; 19:11-12).

When this is compared with James 5:13-16, it is clear that the James passage relates primarily to "gifts of healing" and not necessarily to "effecting of miracles," the former being standard procedure in the function of the church.

The Reverend Joseph Ellison, in a sermon on the potency of faith, gives helpful insight with regard to the gifts of healing.

> There are human healings, either through a physician or otherwise, but there is also a Divine Healing, what is called here "the gifts of healing" (plural) for there are no two healings alike and no two methods alike by which they are reached. The Lord does not grant healing mechanically, every case must be taken as a separate case to Him and be dealt with separately by Him.[1]

The gift of healing in the scriptural sense is not an office but an occurrence. The use of the plural makes each case of healing a bestowment of a gift. R. C. H. Lenski explains the significance of the plural:

> The plural of the governing noun as well as the plural of its genitive are significant and indicate that all healings and all miracles are in each separate case gifts.[2]

From Paul's language it appears that neither the apostles

nor the early Christians created a category of "healers" in the church. The gifts of physical healing were manifested in the assembly without emphasis on the human instrument.

Henry Alford's treatment of the plural usage in First Corinthians 12:28-30 is as follows:

> The apostle has above placed the concrete *apostoloi, prophetai, didaskaloi* in opposition with *dunanaeis* and *charisma iamaton* and now proceeds with the same arrangement till he comes to *charismata iamaton* which being too palpably unpredictable of persons gives rise to the change of construction.[3]

Care must be taken when drawing conclusions from the above fact. No doubt the charisma of healing works through human instrumentality. The instructions relative to the anointing of the sick, the laying on of hands, and the prayer of faith certify the place of the servant of God in the ministry of healing who served as a channel for the bestowing of divine healing even without awareness.

It seems as though the Holy Spirit anticipated the inherent dangers of such a spectacular charisma as being in the capacity of an individual to bring physical healing. God cannot be used for one's own purposes. Any predilection of this tendency is not only presumptuous but also destructive because it arouses false expectations and contributes to the ultimate loss of faith in God.

Perhaps one of the greatest dangers is the possibility and danger of self-aggrandizing careers in which sensationalism replaces spirituality and healing is emphasized out of all proportion to other important aspects of the gospel ministry. In the interest of effecting a cure, the moral factor in illness is easily overlooked and the patient is encouraged to focus on results rather than on Christ.

Furthermore, the important aspect of healing by "signs and wonders" through God's special providences is not properly distinguished from healing as "the children's bread." Such a loss of distinction causes the church to lose the identity of its message within the world and Christianity is potentially degenerated into magic and cultism. A disproportionate emphasis on healing tends to equate illness with lack of faith or sin and to identify falsely both faith and health.

The Greek consistently uses the plural form three times for each of the gift occurrences regarding healings and miracles. These occur in the plural while all others are in the singular—likely because they are subject to abuse by those who use them for public spectacle and for self-aggrandizement.

But great and grave as these dangers are, there is equal danger of limiting the power of God to work in the church and through dedicated instruments.

Few reliable men in modern times have dared to claim the gift of healing. Perhaps the most renown of these was Pastor Blumhardt of Germany. His biography has this to say about the "charisma" manifest in his fruitful ministry.

> He possessed a keenness of spiritual insight that judged, with rarely mistaken accuracy, whether the removal or the continuance of the disease would be in accord with the will of God. He held that this discerning faculty was a "charisma," a gift of God. . . . It was bestowed for gracious purposes of divine pity toward sufferers; it could never be arbitrarily assumed, and where it has been given it was not to be slighted or neglected. He said to one, "You, as a student of theology, know the gifts of healing were frequent in apostolic times. I was not aware that the gift was intended for me. I had not asked for it; rather, I accepted it with fear and trembling." Even possessed with this gift, he carefully guarded all persons from any impression that it was merely by laying on hands or by any physical exertion that cures came. "My remedy," he invariably said, "is simply prayer."[4]

This testimony bears out the emphasis that the human instrument, employed by the Spirit in the exercise of charismatic gifts, must be kept in the background. It further gives an important insight into the nature of the gift itself. Blumhardt did not lay claim to special powers, but in the exercise of the gift of healing he employed the essential law of prevailing prayer. He refused to cultivate a mystique about the gift.

The will and sovereignty of God

The gifts of healings are evidently governed by both the will and the sovereignty of God. The general statements regarding the use of charismatic endowments apply to the exercise of the gifts of healing just as they do to the other gifts. The Scripture says:

> But one and the same Spirit works all these things, distributing to each one individually as He wills (1 Cor. 12:11).

Verse 28 implies the sovereignty of God in the bestowing and, subsequently, in the use of the gifts. God appoints gifts in the church for His own purpose. It is unfortunate that some have assumed that to have a gift is to have unlimited exercise of that gift. Divine wisdom has provided certain checks to avoid this error. Gifts are to be exercised in conformity with the purpose of God.

The interrelationship of several gifts

The gift of faith, the gift of miracles, the gift of showing mercy—all are related to the scriptural doctrine of physical healing. Faith is the only spiritual quality which is both a fruit of the Spirit and a gift of the Spirit. All

Christians have exercised faith, or they could not be saved. The principle of living for Christ is stated by Paul:

> *The righteous man shall live by faith* (Rom. 1:17; Gal. 3:11).

Faith

A mature believer having become Spirit-filled learns a higher level of faith. He develops, under the teaching of the Holy Spirit, the fruit of faith. But above and beyond saving faith and the fruit of faith is the gift of faith. Not all of God's children can claim this gift.

Hebrews 11 records multiplied cases of the incredible happening in response to faith. Not everything in Hebrews 11 is the gift of faith, for the chapter offers a much broader treatment. The summary in verses 30-39 gives some concrete examples of the gift of faith at work.

At least three references in Hebrews 11 relate to the truth of physical healing. Sarah was given the ability to conceive and give birth to Isaac, the son of promise, by a very high level of faith. This miracle of divine life at work quickening a human body was the result of the gift of faith. Sarah was enabled to believe God for the impossible!

The weak were made strong by faith. Samson supplies an example of an ordinary man being quickened with strength for God's glory. Moses was made strong and Caleb experienced the same thing. These ancient men of God received physical strength by faith.

Women received back their dead by resurrection (v. 35) no doubt refers to the raising of the son of the widow of Sarepta by the prophet Elijah. The raising of the dead in both Testaments may be categorized as a healing process. Those individuals raised from the dead were not immortal and became subject to death again. Their recovery was a physical quickening from the Spirit of God that restored the bodily functions once more. What they experienced more accurately resembles healing than it does the bodily change effected by the final resurrection.

In modern times the gift of faith has been manifest in men such as George Müller of Bristol. By faith Müller established a ministry with orphan children that took an enormous sum of money. He refused to make public his needs, operating on the principle that God would supply these needs in response to faith. The published narratives of Müller's adventures in faith read like a chapter in the book of Acts. Among the exploits of the gift of faith in this man was a remarkable ministry of healing.

George Müller experienced physical healing in answer to prayer but suffered ill health during much of his ministry. Müller was not dogmatic on the subject of healing, but by naked faith laid hold of God many times for personal healing and especially for the healing of others. A. T. Pierson says of Müller:

> He observed that repeatedly he prayed with the sick until they were restored, he asking unconditionally for the blessing of bodily health, a thing which he says, later on, he could not have done. Almost always in such cases the petition was granted, yet in some instances not.[5]

The healings under Müller no doubt were the fruit of the gift of faith. It may be that the gift of faith is particularly needed in very stubborn and chronic cases of illness.

Miracles

The gift of effecting miracles falls into that category of gifts having to do with healing. The same Greek word *dunamis* is used of healings performed by Christ during

His earthly ministry. The gift of miracles seems to be a special charisma for dealing with mental disorders and demon possession.

The ninth chapter of Luke offers evidence of such a usage of *dunamis.* The raising of the dead would be another effect of this gift. The gift of effecting miracles cannot be limited to extraordinary cures of mental and physical conditions. It is a word frequently used for miracles demonstrating the greatness of God's power.

Showing mercy

The gift of showing mercy is mentioned by Paul in Romans 12:8:

> *He who shows mercy [let him exercise it], with cheerfulness.*

Perhaps the most prevalent use of this gift is in ministry to the sick. The visitation of the sick is an art. Some pastors and lay people have, under the operation of the Holy Spirit, developed a gift for this essential ministry. The therapy brought about by a proper visit to the sick is in one sense healing. People are often frustrated, tense, confused, and extremely irritated during a time of physical illness. To be able to bring them encouragement and some degree of relief from their mental attitude is a great ministry.

The gift of showing mercy, the Bible says, is to be exercised in a climate of cheerfulness. The kind of cheerfulness of which Paul speaks is most often found in a broken heart. The gift of mercy comes most often to those who know much about the way of suffering. They have empathy with the sick that does not have to be explained. It is just there.

The practical side of the gift of showing mercy ought not to be overlooked. Those who minister in this Spirit-taught way do more for the patient by their actions than by their words. To read to the patient, wash his hair, write a letter, or do one of a score of tasks the patient is not able to perform for himself is an act of mercy the sufferer can see. The loving ministry of a Christian friend means much in such an hour of need.

The newer evangelical church bodies that teach healing have been very weak regarding this gift. For the most part it has been entirely overlooked as a part of the church's healing ministry. Deacons and deaconesses should covet this gift, as they are often engaged in the visitation of the sick. Members of the church engaged in the medical professions may well long for this gift; they have every right to claim spiritual gifts that will make them more effective servants of Christ in their professions.

Helps

A fourth gift associated with the church's ministry of healing, the *gift of helps,* comes from the Greek term *antilempseis,* meaning "to take upon oneself the burden of another." Those members of the body of Christ with this gift concern themselves with ministry to the sick, the poor, and the troubled in mind and heart.

J. R. Pridie of Cambridge, writing on the gift of helps, says:

> But if they be translated—as they quite rightly may be—"nursing" wise guiding, they complete and amplify the gifts of healings, and suggest not only different powers of help entrusted to different persons, but also thoughtful and informed counsel as to the kind of healing to be employed in any particular case.[6]

There is evidence that *antilempseis* had a medical connotation. The gift of nursing sick people was given in the early church and without a doubt is bestowed in modern times.

Healing as a work of Christ's church is dependent upon the gifts of the Holy Spirit distributed in the assembly of believers. These gifts are in the church, though little used and little understood. Serious study and prayerful consideration should be given the above gifts by any church which seeks to be a true New Testament church.

Church health and healing

Gifts of healing must be seen not in isolation from other gifts but as belonging to the full ministry of the church. Healing is related to the health of the church and the redemption of the whole human personality. To put physical needs before the spiritual is to reverse God's order; to emphasize gifts of healings without regard for the plenum of God's gifts is to distort the message and the image of the church. A holy church is a healthy church that holds things in balance and in proper relationship.

The recognized procedures in James 5 involve the entire church in the healing process. To *call for the elders* is to call for the leaders in the local body of Christ. Carrying out the instruction *confess your sins to one another, and pray for one another, so that you may be healed* is a church affair. Healing takes place in an organism in which each member is related to every other member in vital spiritual service. The gifts are given and distributed to the church by the Holy Spirit; individuals participate in the gifts through the church.

When James writes "pray for one another, so that you

may be healed" (v. 16), he uses the same Greek word for *pray* that is translated "wish" in Romans 9:3:

> *For I could wish that I myself were accursed, sepa-*
> *rated from Christ for the sake of my brethren, my*
> *kinsmen according to the flesh.*

And, again, when John wrote to Gaius, "Beloved, I pray (*wish*, KJ) that in all respects you may prosper and be in good health, just as your soul prospers" (3 John 2), the same word is used. The instruction *pray for one another* is more than generalized praying; it is empathy and agony of soul born out of mutual burden bearing in the love of Christ and in the body of Christ.

The functionality of the gifts is not designed for each individual to suit himself. Healing, never an end in itself, is a spiritual blessing before it is a mere physical one. It becomes a source of strength and produces power to serve Christ in and through the church.

Spiritual healing will come primarily as a result of prayer, biblical knowledge, faith, and the working of the Holy Spirit in and through the body of Christ. God in His sovereignty desires to work in the context of utter simplicity without wanton publicity. But in spite of inexperience, in spite of inadequacy, in spite of the danger of misunderstanding and disappointments, it is a ministry the church should offer in loving concern to the glory of God. It is the "children's bread."

---

[1] Joseph Ellison, "The Faith of God," *Overcomer,* April 1932, p. 24.

[2] R. C. H. Lenski, *The Interpretation of St. Paul's First and Second Epistles to the Corinthians,* p. 502.

[3] Henry Alford, *The Greek New Testament,* 2:584.

[4] *Pastor Blumhardt,* pp. 91-92.

[5] A. T. Pierson, *George Müller of Bristol,* p. 89.

[6] J. R. Pridie, *The Church's Ministry of Healing,* p. 63.

9

Divine Healing
and Demon Possession

FOR TOO LONG CHURCH theologians have looked
upon the exorcising of evil spirits as a relic of primitive
mentality which modern development and knowledge have
conquered. Modern Satan worship, spiritism, and the
popularity of astrology have brought a new awareness of
paganism in North America; shock waves from the movie
"The Exorcist" are still with us.

The truth is that demons do exist and do enter and control human personalities. The validity of the exorcist, however, is often confused with the credibility of divine healing. Both exorcism and divine healing have been mis-
understood by people predominantly influenced by naturalism and humanism.

Any interpretation of divine truth must be tested by
principles of understanding which support a total view of
divine revelation as found in the Scriptures. Sin has dark-
ened the understanding of man and the powers of evil
exercise pernicious influence on the conscious mental life

of people. Wherever Satan and demonic activity are exposed, there confusion and distortion will be prevalent unless strong counteraction is taken.

The naturalist mentality

Naturalism is not of modern origin; it began with Adam and Eve in the Garden of Eden when Satan said: "You surely shall not die! For God knows that in the day you eat from it your eyes will be opened, and you will be like God, knowing good and evil" (Gen. 3:4-5). Naturalism asserts that man can take a position independent from God and can determine good from evil for himself.

The Greek philosophers five centuries before Christ believed they could discover ultimate reality and whatever gods there were. According to modern naturalism, we can know only that which can be proved with our senses or with scientific data; the universe is confined to that which we observe by using the discoverable laws of cause and effect.

Though this philosophy is not explicitly taught openly, its presuppositions are generally assumed in the modern classroom and in various media.

Christians do believe in the uniformity of natural laws, but to them the cosmos is not a closed system and God cannot be confined in it. In the long run, Christianity alone makes technology possible, in terms of its view of an ordered universe and all that is implied. It is not incidental that modern technology developed after the Renaissance and the Reformation.

There are two parts to reality; beyond the natural world there is a supernatural universe of both good and evil. There is an evil spirit world with power to enter man who volitionally invites such spirits; but beyond this, there is a heaven where love, goodness, and ultimate and absolute truth dwell with the eternal God.

The Christian is called upon to demonstrate in history that the supernatural world exists, particularly that God not only exists but that He is both immanent and transcendent. Secularism is the refusal to let God be God. It denies the relevance of Christianity to the major concerns of life and preoccupies itself with interests other than loyalty to God and warfare against Satan and his spirits.

The need to understand demonology

The modern scene calls for a fresh look at biblical demonology as it relates to the everyday life and ministry of the church. For many years evangelical Christians have been willing to accept the fact of demon possession in pagan cultures, but have been almost totally unaware of the presence and work of evil spirits in Christian nations.

The devil is smart enough to adapt stratagems to the enlightenment of the age, but changes that have come about in the culture of the twentieth century are such that demonism is now as prevalent in the so-called Christian countries as in many non-Christian countries. It seems incredible that witchcraft, sorcery, divination, astrology, and other forms of mediumistic contact with evil spirits should be so widely practiced in Western civilization, but anyone who is knowledgeable of Western culture today knows that demonism is enjoying an enormous revival. It is estimated that there are at least four hundred full-time spiritists in New York City alone.

This increase in demonism is a natural result of the basic philosophy of humanism and naturalism that has governed man's thinking in much of the Western world in the last hundred years. Because of the vacuum that results when man becomes his own god, he has little alternative but to turn back to the devil. He begins to worship the powers of darkness and to seek the supernatural through this medium rather than to recognize the supernatural power of the true creator God.

Not too many years ago theologians were questioning whether or not demonism was actually a reality. Even those who were somewhat conservative in their theological position were of the opinion that Christ may have been compromising at this point with the ignorance of His day. That He looked upon mental disorder and psychological problems as the work and activity of evil spirits.

An inductive study of the New Testament Scripture disproves this position. Christ clearly made a distinction between mental illness and demon possession. The phenomena and activity of demon possession were explicitly given in the New Testament Scriptures.

It is important that the church restudy her doctrine and also her practice with regard to the phenomena of demon possession. Although a great rarity a few years ago, now pastors, elders, Sunday school workers, and youth workers are constantly encountering what apparently are strong cases of oppression and, in many instances, actual possession. Anyone who has an extensive ministry in today's culture needs a working knowledge of biblical demonology and the biblical practice of exorcism. He may have no need greater than the ability to recognize the devices of Satan.

Defining exorcism as distinct from healing

Exorcism and healing are not one and the same thing. They are closely related, and both rest upon the finished work of Christ and the authority invested in the church through the name of the Lord Jesus Christ. When Jesus sent out the twelve, He "gave them power and authority over all the demons, and to heal diseases" (Luke 9:1). The same Scriptures that authorize the church to heal authorize the church to also cast out spirits in the name of the Lord Jesus (Mark 16:17-18; Acts 8:7; 16:18; 19:11-12).

Church history shows that in ancient times the church practiced exorcism extensively. In the third century when most of the church's converts were from paganism, it was common practice that an exorcist would minister to the new converts alongside the catechist. One would teach them Christian doctrine, the other would deal with any existing ground for the possession and activity of evil spirits in their lives. Prior to their baptism, converts were not only taught doctrine but were thoroughly delivered from every vestige of their worship and devotion to the evil spirits. When infant baptism was first practiced, the catechumen's preparatory acts were combined into the liturgy of baptism and exorcism became an integral part of the rite.

Before exploring the biblical teachings of the practice of exorcism the reader should have in mind a clear definition of demon possession. It is only fair to say that there are mental and nervous disorders that are not demon possession. Unfortunately, extreme viewpoints have been held by some, indicating that all mental illness has an evil spirit at its source. Mental illness could be due to some physical disorder or some weakness and, therefore, cannot necessarily be attributed to an evil spirit.

Christ is able to heal mental illness just as He is able to heal physical illness. It is appropriate to anoint and pray for the mentally ill that they may recover. Remarkable incidents can be cited of healings in answer to prayer for those with mental and nervous disorders.

Demon possession is a condition that may have the outward appearance of mental disturbance and nervous disorder, but the activity of a personal evil spirit is the source of the problem. The condition of demon possession does not come about as an accident. The evil spirits have intelligence and are capable of communication. These disembodied spirits are personalities. They seek to inhabit a human personality and, because they are fallen and wicked by nature, seek to emphasize their particular kind of wickedness in the personality they have been able to overcome.

In theological language the cause of the possession is termed "the ground." The ground of possession is that particular sin that has such a hold over the individual that ultimately the evil spirit is able to claim dominion of the personality through the practice of this particular sin. Although there are many grounds of demon possession, the four most dominant are the practice of spiritism, excessive anger, sexual sins, and pride.

It is not uncommon for the habitation of an evil spirit in the human personality to produce physical illness. The New Testament mentions demons that caused epilepsy, deafness and dumbness, and, in one instance, even the suggestion that fever was caused by an evil spirit.

In an earlier chapter it was discussed—but we need to refer to it again—that demons are capable of causing physical illness. However, physical illnesses directly due to the dominion of an evil spirit over the individual are not the rule but the exception.

It is common for the victim to show dullness with regard to anything spiritual—almost a total failure to comprehend spiritual truth. Quite often there is psychological disturbance. It is important that those who seek to deal with demon possession exercise every care in determining whether or not the individual is actually possessed. Great harm can be done by attempting to deal with a physical and mental condition as though it were demon possession. Such a ministry should be undertaken not by novices, but by experienced and gifted believers. Certainly pastors and elders of the church should give themselves to the study of the biblical teaching with regard to demonism and exorcism.

The stages of demon activity

There are several stages of demon activity, each representing a little deeper penetration of the human personality. Demon possession is the most intense stage and represents a takeover of a personality. Demon activity may take the form of an attack or it may be in the form of oppression or depression of spirit. Evil spirits will then seek to use the tactic of obsession. This strategy is to convince the individual of a lie and to urge him to become so obsessed with the lie that it controls his life. This is a more advanced degree of demon domination over the personality, often leading quite rapidly to a full state of possession.

Those who undertake exorcism should understand these stages and learn to discern between them. If the individual is possessed, there is often violent resistance to any effort to exorcise the spirit or to drive it out of its place of dominion. Physical violence is not uncommon. Such individuals may go into convulsions, froth at the mouth, or become extremely strong and attempt to do physical violence to those who are carrying on the ministry of exorcism, as described in Acts 19:13-16.

Keeping perspective

For those who undertake the ministry of exorcism, a

key passage is found in Luke 10. Christ appointed seventy disciples to go out two by two to minister in the cities. They were given instruction to proclaim the gospel and to heal the sick. They later reported to Him the effectiveness of their ministry and were greatly impressed with the fact that in the name of Jesus even the evil spirits fled. Luke 10:17-20 reads:

> *And the seventy returned with joy, saying, "Lord, even the demons are subject to us in Your name." And He said to them, "I was watching Satan fall from heaven like lightning. Behold, I have given you authority to tread upon serpents and scorpions, and over all the power of the enemy, and nothing shall injure you. Nevertheless do not rejoice in this, that the spirits are subject to you, but rejoice that your names are recorded in heaven."*

The Lord Jesus implied that all who are involved in the ministry of exorcism should exercise care to keep it in perspective. The tendency to become extreme, to see demons everywhere and in everything, and to devote one's whole time to the expelling of evil spirits is unhealthy and unwise —a course to be resisted. An exorcist must rejoice that he is a child of God and that the name of the Lord Jesus Christ is that power by which the enemy is defeated.

Verse 19 contains the credentials of the exorcists:

> *"Behold, I have given you authority to tread upon serpents and scorpions, and over all the power of the enemy, and nothing shall injure you."*

It is quite common for Satan to attack those who must deal in the ministry of exorcism with intense fear, the fear of counterattack or possession or some other kind of fear. This is most devastating, often keeping an individual from exercising such a ministry. Jesus made it clear that He conferred this power upon the church, that it is proper, and that all the power of His mighty name rests behind it. The child of God whose heart is right and who is obedient to the Lord need not fear the enemy in carrying out this ministry. He stands upon the ground of divine authority and the enemy knows this full well.

A ministry of exorcism should be preceded by much heart searching and prayer. Time given to the study of Scripture will assure that the whole procedure is based upon the Word of God and upon the triumph of the Lord Jesus Christ over all the forces of darkness.

Before His ascension into heaven, Jesus said to His disciples:

> *"And these signs will accompany those who believe: in My name they will cast out demons"* (Mark 16:17a).

This statement indicates that the ministry of exorcism will continue throughout the church age.

Without a doubt there have been periods in the history of Christian nations when the need was not great, but we are moving into a period when the need is great. Many people in our culture have had traffic with evil spirits and are affected in one way or another by them. One who is evangelizing and working in such a culture must be prepared to meet the problem of demon possession and other forms of demon activity. He must know how to deal with it. He must realize the great victory of the Lord Jesus Christ, the fact that in His name there is deliverance today just as in the day of the early church.

The problem of witchcraft and demonism in Great Britain is so serious that some Anglican church leaders have advocated that an exorcist be appointed in every congregation. The condition in North America is little better.

It is hardly likely that a pastor will work many weeks or months without coming into contact with some form of demonism in his own congregation. The various subcultures in our society today have given thousands of people exposure directly to spiritism. The use of drugs, certain practices of yoga, and various forms of meditation which create a passive state of mind open the personality to evil spirits.

The philosophy of existentialism has created a favorable climate for the mediumistic. When the rational is dismissed from the processes of religion, man is then left with the emotional and the psychic. This condition has produced a wave of counterfeit religious experiences. Experience-oriented cults are multiplying. Some areas of the contemporary charismatic movement show mediumistic tendencies. Many people are coming under the dominion of evil spirits in the seeking of false religious experience.

Procedures in the ministry of exorcism

Not only has our Lord commissioned His church to carry out a ministry of exorcism, but He has also instructed the church and equipped the church for the exercise of such a ministry. The gifts of the Holy Spirit are designed to help those who must carry out this work.

The first essential gift for the ministry of exorcism is that of discernment. There must be those who, by the study of the Word and obedience to the Holy Spirit, have developed a very keen sensitivity and are able to identify cases of possession. We are instructed in the Scripture not to believe every spirit, but to try whether the spirits are of God.

Suspicious religious manifestations should not be accepted but rather tested and tried. In First John 4:1-3a the apostle says:

> *Beloved, do not believe every spirit, but test the spirits to see whether they are from God; because many false prophets have gone out into the world. By this you know the Spirit of God: every spirit that confesses that Jesus Christ has come in the flesh is from God; and every spirit that does not confess Jesus is not from God.*

We are as much in need of this exhortation as was the primitive church.

If the physical, psychic, and mental activity of the individual is suspicious, the spirit should then be tested to determine whether or not the source is demonic. John gives the key for carrying out such a test.

At the time of the manifestation the individual in charge should address the spirit with this question: Did Jesus Christ come in the flesh? It is shocking to hear a voice answer back an emphatic, "No!" Such an answer makes it obvious that an evil spirit is in charge of this individual. Immediately the exorcist should take steps to expel the evil spirit.

While the procedure from this point may vary, it is a good practice to ascertain the name of the evil spirit. This was the method used by the Lord Jesus quite frequently. By calling for the name of the spirit, one generally learns whether it is a multiple or single possession. Often the name indicates the ground or that particular sin in the individual's life on which the possession rests. To expose this is to weaken greatly the position of the evil spirit.

The final procedure is to command the evil spirit to leave in the name of the Lord Jesus Christ. This should be done emphatically and boldly, realizing that Christ has absolute authority. The evil spirit has no authority at all; all the ground and authority he has taken, he has usurped. The spirit world knows this fact and recognizes when Christians understand this and take their stand on the ground of Christ's finished work.

Special instructions

Having two or three individuals dealing with a case of possession is a good practice. Each of them should be well prepared, having prayed and sought the Scriptures and equipped themselves for this particular battle. Spectators at such a procedure bring confusion. It is dangerous to have children or unbelievers present.

For the most part, possession should not be dealt with in public meetings. An exception would be that when a manifestation occurs in a public meeting, it may be necessary to deal with it at that very time. Generally, it can be handled in a private session.

In most cases the individual is not aware of the fact that he is possessed. In the proceedings of prayer and the manifestation of demon activity the individual begins to understand what his condition is. Those who carry out the ministry of exorcism should then instruct the individual, counsel with him, and urge him to cooperate in every way in order to bring full relief from his condition.

It is a healthy practice that when the individual is rational to have him pray and to distinctly renounce any and all affiliation with the evil spirits that possess him. Failure of the individual to cooperate will hinder the process and sometimes render it impossible to bring about deliverance. The individual should be carefully instructed about the death of Christ, the meaning of the blood, and the repentance and renouncing of sin. He should be urged to call on the Lord for salvation.

The doctrine of the Lordship of Christ is part and parcel of any true presentation of the gospel, and it is extremely important in the lives of those people who have surrendered the government of their personality to an evil spirit. Deliverance calls for an act of their will to renounce the lordship of Satan over them and to receive without question the unreserved Lordship of the Lord Jesus Christ over every part of their spirit, soul, and body.

Pastors and elders and other mature Christians that undertake this ministry must understand that there may be excessive manifestations at the time the evil spirit leaves. The body may be distorted; there may be convulsions, loud screaming. Those in charge must remain very calm and persist in declaring the power of the Lord Jesus Christ. Excessive manifestation is often done by the enemy to impress the exorcist and to attempt to frighten him and get him to back off. One must stand the ground in Jesus' name and claim through the power of the blood of Christ complete victory.

It helps to have a band of praying people that are exercising the ministry of intercession simultaneously with the efforts to bring deliverance. The power to bind, in the name of Christ, has been given to His servants. Remarkable results have come when those in charge command the evil spirit, in the name of Jesus, to become quiet and to go quietly. The influence and power of the evil spirits may be bound by the exercise of faith on the part of the believers.

Another precaution should be taken with regard to the efforts of evil spirits to engage the exorcists in conversation. This strategy to delay the deliverance is not healthy for the exorcist. It can be assumed that the enemy has no truth. All the truth the people of God need is found in Jesus Christ and in the revealed Scriptures. The only accurate and trustworthy information on Satan and his activity is to be found within the Bible. It is often the device of evil spirits to attempt to give information and to engage the exorcist in such conversation that it becomes mediumistic. Every care should be exercised to avoid this. Just persist in singing, praying, quoting Scripture, and commanding the evil spirits to leave in the name of Christ.

Not all cases of demon possession are vocal and violent. There are dumb spirits that never speak. These may be dealt with in a similar pattern, and one knows that deliverance has come by the fact that the individual is released from the condition or manifestation that attended his possession.

Lessons from examples

The writer dealt with a case of a girl who had been engaging in mediumistic practices, which resulted in her having seizures. The plan of salvation was presented to her, she accepted the Lord Jesus Christ as Savior and renounced the ground she had given in her life to the evil spirit. A group of us then engaged in prayer, followed by commanding the evil spirit to leave her. There was no outward indication. A seizure came upon her during prayer; after commanding the evil spirit to leave, the seizure stopped and she never had another. She was delivered from that moment on.

Another case of which the author is acquainted, a young wife had used a Ouija board extensively; after becoming a Christian the thought occurred to use it as a means of guidance by the Holy Spirit. The result was that she began to have rather strange attacks that came upon her without warning. Her husband had to be called at work to come and get her when such an attack occurred while she was grocery shopping. The evil spirit causing these attacks was identified by discerning Christians, and after prayer she immediately went into a convulsion and the evil spirit was commanded to leave. She was released within minutes. She has had freedom of spirit since and has been growing and maturing in her spiritual life.

The writer has also experienced dealing with cases of possession that resulted from the seeking of a physical evidence of speaking in tongues. In two separate incidents that have occurred in my ministry, both individuals were falsely instructed regarding the Holy Spirit. By insisting on speaking in tongues they opened themselves up to invasion of the evil spirits. The result was identical in both lives. They suffered from an intense spirit of fear, uncontrollable manifestations, and a total devastation of spiritual life. When the evil spirit was identified and cast out, they were delivered and enjoyed recovery spiritually.

The extensive need of our day

In contemporary society there is a veritable occult explosion. Universities are offering classes in witchcraft. Witches are practicing in most nations. Satanism is now a form of organized religion with churches in several North American major cities. The widespread use of the horoscope indicates that a high percentage of the population depends on it for guidance. It would not be such a great problem if this were a simple superstition, but it is an overt practice of spirit worship. It is the surrender of the human personality to supernatural forces outside himself in an effort to resolve problems and to learn about his future.

Both the Old and New Testament Scriptures warn of the danger of such a practice. The beginning of occultism was very early in human society. The Tower of Babel was no doubt its genesis, for the word for *tower* in the original language is identified with the zodiac. It appears that men at this early period, having renounced God's will and way, were seeking a supernatural power to take its place.

Man's cry for the supernatural reveals his deep need. When he has turned God down, he has nowhere else to go but to the evil spirits. The post-Christian culture of the Western world has nowhere to go but to the occult. It is in this kind of climate that modern evangelicals are called upon to preach the gospel. It is relevant in our time that those who proclaim the gospel of Jesus Christ be prepared to cast out demons and to heal the sick, for the needs in present-day society are the same as existed in the society in which Jesus and His apostles lived.

The general ignorance of the Bible in our day leaves the culture wide open to the activity of the evil spirits. Young people from a Christian home and an evangelical church, when having a slumber party, have been known to use Ouija boards and to practice other forms of mediumistic activity without even being aware of their danger. It indicates total ignorance of the vast amount of Bible teaching on this subject.

The Old Testament contains a list of the various activities of the occult and warns of their danger.

> *As for a man or a woman, if there is a medium or a spiritist among them, they shall surely be put to death; they shall be stoned with stones, their blood-guiltiness is upon them* (Lev. 20:27).

God has dealt severely with the spiritist throughout biblical history. Deuteronomy 18:12 states the intense judgment that came upon the Canaanite nations because of their abominable practices of the occult. God judged them by total destruction of their cultures and by giving their land to another people. Verses 10-11 list mediumistic activities:

> *"There shall not be found among you anyone who makes his son or his daughter pass through the fire, one who uses divination, one who practices witch-craft, or one who interprets omens, or a sorcerer, or one who casts a spell, or a medium, or a spiritist, or one who calls up the dead."*

Virtually every one of these practices can be found in both Western and Eastern cultures.

Responsible church leadership can no longer keep the doctrine of demonology on the academic level. The time has come when the church must again practice exorcism in the name of the Lord Jesus Christ. The ministry of deliverance is part and parcel of any contemporary effort to preach Jesus Christ.

Follow-up and continued healing

The ministry of exorcism does not cease with the driving out of the evil spirit. This traumatic experience leaves the individual with a need for the healing of his total personality. Acts 10:38 says that Jesus went about healing those who were oppressed of the devil. The delivered victim ought to be carefully taught and instructed in those provisions of the Lord Jesus for his continued victory. There ought to be prayer and counseling to aid him in a healing of the whole person that he may become an effective follower of the Lord Jesus Christ and live an overcoming life through the victory of the cross and the resurrection.

It is of interest that Luke, the Greek physician, gives such detail about the cure of those possessed by demons. He uses medical terminology in describing their cures.

And those who were troubled with unclean spirits were cured (Luke 6:18).

And while he was still approaching, the demon dashed him to the ground, and threw him into a violent convulsion. But Jesus rebuked the unclean spirit, and healed the boy, and gave him back to his father (9:42).

The deliverance in each of these cases is spoken of as a healing. The casting out of an evil spirit and the subsequent restoration of the mind and body are a healing process. The benefit of exorcism could be lost by the failure to seek a healing of those mental and physical effects of the possession.

The frequent mention in the Epistles of the conflict with demons proves both their existence and their continued activity until the close of the present age. These organized spirit personalities make consistent war upon all the efforts of gospel ministry and upon the daily walk of every Christian. A part of victorious living is to be aware of this spiritual conflict and to know what divine provision has been made for overcoming the enemy.

The Lord Jesus Christ confronted Satan and all the powers of darkness in His Calvary death. Paul fully captured this great encounter when he wrote:

And when you were dead in your transgressions and the uncircumcision of your flesh, He made you alive together with Him, having forgiven us all our transgressions, having cancelled out the certificate of debt consisting of decrees against us and which was hostile to us; and He has taken it out of the way, having nailed it to the cross. When He had disarmed the rulers and authorities, He made a public display of

them having triumphed over them through Him (Col.
2:13-15).

The death of Christ broke the power of sin in the flesh
and took Satan's ground from him. The blood of Christ
is the greatest single power available to the churches in
withstanding the forces of darkness.

John says in Revelation 12:11a:

> *"And they overcame him because of the blood of the
> Lamb."*

All believers need this instruction, but it is especially needed
by those delivered from possession or other form of enemy
assault.

10

Divine Healing and Modern Medicine

THE CHURCH HAS BEEN both commissioned and endowed to minister the *charisma* of healing. Christians today have difficulty relating the church's ministry of healing to modern medicine. Are divine healing and modern medicine mutually exclusive? With great hospitals, wonder drugs, surgery, and new therapies, why should the church concern itself with healing?

The questions raised by the tension between medicine and supernatural healing are not new. As early as the second century, the controversy between the church and medicine was underway. Greek medicine reached its peak at the very time Christianity was spreading across southern Europe. The successful, nonmiraculous healing by means of drugs gave the church concern.

Though the church took a negative view of medicine in most instances, it did minister to the sick in ways other than the exercise of the gift of healing. The popularization of Christianity under the Roman emperor Constantine created a spiritual climate for the institutionalizing of healing. Fabiola established the first hospital. Basil of Caesarea opened a leprosarium. Thalasias started an asylum for the blind. A merchant named Apollionius provided the first free dispensary.

The church's charismatic healing ministry existed alongside a growing number of institutional ministries to physical needs. While the science of medicine came to maturity in the secular world, most of the essential institutions for the care of the sick came from the church. They are the products of Spirit-motivated compassion for the sick and suffering.

Since the second century, Christians have reacted in one of two ways to the use of medical means by a believer. Origen (A.D. 185-253) was of the opinion that divine healing without the aid of medicine was the superior way of healing. Origen said,

> When one seeks help in illness it is possible to use the usual and simple method of medicine. It is also possible to use the higher and better way and seek blessing from Him who is God above all, and seek Him in devotion and prayer.[1]

Other church fathers protested the materialistic approach of medicine. The controversy became so heated that the church pressured Justinian (A.D. 527-567) to close the medical schools at Athens and Alexandria. In the year 1215 Pope Innocent III condemned surgery, and in 1248 the church determined that the dissection of the human body was a sacrilege. The church's controversy with the science of medicine prevailed until modern times.

Since the beginning of the modern healing movement, which dates from the middle of the nineteenth century, a number of Bible teachers have espoused the viewpoint that to trust God for healing necessitates the putting aside of all medical assistance. There has not been agreement among

Bible teachers on this point. The answer to the controversy is a careful study of the Scriptures to determine what they actually say about medicine as a science.

Bible view of the physician

The Bible does not prohibit the Christian from consulting a physician or using medical means in the treatment of illness, nor does it specifically state that the use of natural means is a deterent to faith for divine healing. While this has been the contention of many, let us allow the Bible to speak for itself at this point.

On one occasion found in the Old Testament Scriptures, Asa was rebuked by God for consulting a physician. The end result of such a course of rebellion for him was death. Some important factors in this account are frequently overlooked in its interpretation. Asa did not seek the Lord with regard to his physical need. He turned to the physician as a substitute for the Lord and therein lies his sin. Sickness for the Christian is always a subject of prayer. The Lord must be sought first. The method from that point on may vary according to the Lord's leading.

For most of the history of mankind the science of medicine has been associated with sorcery and witchcraft. Even in modern times the level of medical practice has left much to be desired. In the days of Wesley, many ministers carried on the practice of medicine because the need was great and the doctor ineffective. Adam Clarke, early Methodist writer, devotes considerable space in his Pastor's Manual to matters of health and treatment of illness. For the most part the church's attitude in the past toward medicine has had justifiable grounds.

For the past one hundred years the healing sciences have made remarkable progress. Medicine is now built upon a valid scientific approach. The thinking person can only rejoice at the progress being measured in every area of medicine today. However, one must not lose his objectivity at this point. Even modern medicine suffers serious limitations.

There are still cases today which defy all the therapy of medical science just as was true in Christ's day. Luke 8:43 tells of a woman with an issue of blood who spent all her money on medical treatment to no avail. The author can name at least five individuals in the circle of his acquaintance to whom medicine with all its accomplishments can offer no hope. What pastor does not find himself confronted almost daily with cases of physical and mental illness science has been unable to help? Jesus Christ can cure the incurable. Christ the Healer has no limitations on His ability to heal the human body. It is possible for divine intervention to raise up one whose case is terminal.

The church must not lose sight of this fact if she is to minister effectively to the great needs of suffering people, both in the church and outside the church. It becomes the obligation of the Bible-believing church to proclaim the possibilities of Christ's healing power to the hopeless. Such a proclamation will not always induce faith any more than will every evangelistic sermon preached produce converts. Nevertheless, the whole gospel of Jesus Christ must be declared regardless of the results. The record will show that again and again the seeds of faith planted in hopeless hearts have resulted in miracles of physical renewing.

Medicine has always carried the imprint of the basic presuppositions held by the people who practice it. In ancient times the religious presuppositions of the doctor dictated his whole approach to healing. The stars guided him to herbs for medicine and the spirit world revealed his method of treatment. The doctor of the twentieth century no longer holds to such primitive presuppositions. The extensive system of knowledge on which the modern science of medicine rests comes out of a quest for truth.

To the extent that medicine is a pure science it has uncovered the truth about the human body and its treatment. But we should not overlook the fact that modern doctors also have presuppositions, and these tend to color their practice of medicine. For the most part medicine in our time is studied from a humanistic point of view. If the doctor is a thorough going humanist, his treatment of patients will ignore the fact that his patient has a spiritual nature and that his ailment could have roots in some form of spiritual disorder.

If one accepts fully what the Bible teaches about the nature of man, health and healing cannot be committed entirely to medicine and its related sciences. Since man has a spiritual nature it is not always possible to treat his physical problem and neglect to treat the whole person. If a biblical position is to be maintained, the spiritual problem which may be the underlying cause of the physical malady must be dealt with by those who understand spiritual things. The healing ministry carried out by the church eldership is relevant even in this day of advanced medical treatment.

The doctor who holds to a humanistic philosophy will probably overlook this possibility and seek to treat the condition by drugs or some other therapy. Healing does not come, and the patient becomes both a physical and a spiritual invalid. The recovery of such a case, particularly of the individual who is a Christian, may be found in obeying the command laid down in James 5.

Dr. John Wilkinson, medical superintendent of a Presbyterian Hospital in Kenya, Africa, voices a legitimate concern about the popular concepts of health:

> We can only define health in relation to our concept of man, his nature and purpose. We can only define his well-being when we can define man himself. If we think of man in merely biological terms as an animal, then we shall define his well-being in terms of animal comfort and pleasure. Whilst if we think of man in purely economic terms, we shall define his purpose and well-being in terms of his productive capacity and the resultant state of society. By the same token, since there is a Christian view of man, there is also a Christian understanding of health and well-being. It is in the light of the former that we define the latter and this chapter is an attempt to explore this Christian understanding.[2]

Medical doctors like Dr. Wilkinson who embrace a Christian view of man come to see a Christian view of health. Their practice is broadened to take in the whole man. The spiritual side of man's nature must become a consideration. The doctor looks to the church for assistance in ministry to the spiritual needs of his patients.

The New Testament Scriptures do not seem to reflect any antagonism toward physicians on the part of the early Christians. Colossians 4:14 offers some insight on Paul's attitude toward the medical profession of his day.

Luke, the beloved physician, sends you his greetings.

Luke, the Greek physician, was Paul's companion at the time of the writing of this epistle. He remained with Paul throughout his prison experience and no doubt until the time of his execution. The apostle mentions Luke in his last letter to young Timothy (2 Tim. 4:11). It would seem that if Paul looked upon a physician as a threat to complete trust in Christ for his body, he would have dismissed Luke or would have asked him to abandon his role as a physician. It is significant that at the writing of this letter Paul speaks with deep feeling about his friend, the physician.

After many years of exposure to the teaching of Christ

and the apostles on healing, Luke did not find it inconsistent to continue in his profession as a physician. Apparently, he believed Christian healing and the true science of medicine to be compatible. Luke, an inspired historian, researched more incidents of healing occurring during Christ's earthly life and during the early years of the apostolic church than any other biblical writer. He clearly affirms his faith in the reliability of these incidents of nonphysical healing in the name of the Lord Jesus Christ. On numerous occasions the beloved physician was a witness to the healing ministry of the primitive church.

It seems reasonable to believe that after his conversion Luke ministered for the rest of his life as a consecrated Christian doctor. The fact that Paul lists Luke in Philemon as among his fellow workers does not imply that Luke had become a clergyman. Paul counted many laymen among his fellow workers.

While preaching, Christ used the physicians as illustrations of a spiritual truth. He said, "It is not those who are well who need a physician, but those who are sick" (Luke 5:31). Had Christ looked upon the practice of medicine as unnecessary He would not have made such a generalization as found in the above Scripture. Never once did Christ make a negative statement regarding the physicians of His day. The Savior on this occasion lifted an axiom from the everyday life of the people to teach them a new spiritual concept. He was saying that just as sick people need a physician for the treatment of their ills, so a sinner needs Christ for the healing of his spiritual ills.

Medicine is among those good things God has given to man and is to be received with thanksgiving. God's people recognize that all healing ultimately comes from God. No empirical evidence has been produced by medicine or any other science to nullify that biblical assertion.

The late L. Nelson Bell, a practicing physician and well-known Christian (the father-in-law of Evangelist Billy Graham), writes of his own perception of the relationship of divine healing and medicine:

> In the practice of medicine I have noted again and again that people with a simple trust in Jesus Christ have had an attitude of quietness and peace which has contributed to their physical welfare and that where surgery was performed this seemed to hasten their recovery. I have seen cases where God has directly intervened in the healing of disease, where 'hopeless' cases have been cured when, humanly speaking, everything had failed. These things cause us to see how little we know and understand the sovereign power and grace of God.[3]

What then should be the attitude of a Bible-believing Christian with regard to medical means in the event of sickness? The Scriptures offer a guiding principle:

> *Is anyone among you suffering? Let him pray. . . . Is anyone among you sick? Let him call for the elders of the church* (James 5:13-14).

The first order is to seek the Lord in prayer and to avail oneself of the prayers of the church. The spiritual guidance and illumination of the believer during the crisis of illness are as important as the healing of that illness.

There may be a number of good reasons for consultation with a physician. The Bible has not authorized the church to make diagnosis of disease. Seldom are leaders in the church qualified to determine the nature of the illness. This is the work of a qualified physician. If the doctor discovers an ulcer, he may also discover that the eating habits of the patient and the way he lives are the cause of the illness. The doctor may be able to prescribe a diet or a change in habits that will eliminate the condition. He is qualified to speak on such matters. Why should God perform a supernatural healing in the case of a Christian whose eating habits are making him sick? He needs to learn the laws of healthful diet and observe them.

It is certainly a desirable procedure to have a reputable physician examine the individual who appears to be healed to confirm the validity of the healing. The physician can then take the patient off medication and advise him as to maintaining a good physical condition.

Not all physicians would be willing to cooperate, and for this reason a Christian physician is ideal. The writer has found a working relationship between the church and a Christian doctor to be most desirable. Some people who come to the elders for healing need not only prayer but also medical counsel. By the same token, some patients seek advice of a physician when their real need is for spiritual counsel.

Andrew Murray showed candor in discussing the use of medical means by the believer:

> Does the use of remedies exclude the prayer of faith? To this we believe our reply should be: No, for the experience of a large number of believers testifies that in answer to their prayers God has often blest the use of remedies, and made them a means of healing.[4]

Murray, in substance, is saying that God is Healer and He can heal by any means He chooses. What is essential is that He heals in answer to believing prayer.

S. D. Gordon in his book *Quiet Talks About the Healing Christ* comes to a similar position regarding the use of means and trusting for healing:

> Christ heals through means and the skilled human expert, sometimes. *He heals without these, sometimes.* He heals when the physician frankly confesses his inability to cure. And sometimes He heals by overcoming and counteracting the physician and the means used. Ask Him. He's there by

your side, inside. He's intensely interested. He's eager to tell you what to do. In this He is a true physician, for He advises.[5]

Gordon points out that God does heal without means. It should not be considered fanatical to trust the Lord apart from any medical treatment. Such a stance should not be taken lightly. It should be assumed only after much prayer and searching of the Word of God. This higher way of healing calls for a mature walk with Christ.

---

[1] Alexander Roberts and James Donaldson, eds., *The Ante-Nicene Fathers,* 4:60.

[2] Claude A. Frazier, *Faith Healing: Finger of God? or Scientific Curiosity?,* p. 45.

[3] *Ibid.,* p. 8.

[4] Andrew Murray, *Divine Healing,* p. 80.

[5] S. D. Gordon, *Quiet Talks About the Healing Christ,* p. 82.

11

Healing and
the Faith Factor

THE GOSPEL LOAF contains blessing for the whole man, and divine healing for the body is certainly one of those blessings. It is the believer's privilege to claim the "children's bread." Healing is received by faith, but let it be understood that divine healing is not "faith" healing. The healing of the body is the work of God in response to faith. The popular concept of "faith" healing is really humanistic. It implies that the mental act of believing effects a cure.

The nature of faith

Faith is more than auto-suggestion. It is more than having confidence that there is a possibility of cure. Much that has been called "faith" healing can be explained by the science of psychology. Some clergymen and medical doctors speak of the relationship of faith to physical healing in terms that mean something less than what the Bible means by faith. Faith as described in the New Testament does not heal by its subjective effect. Those who received healing by faith believed Christ had the ability and the willingness to heal. Christ is the effective cause of healing, faith only the instrumental cause. Faith is powerless without the immediate touch of Christ Himself.

The character and perfections of Christ as revealed in the Scripture prompt men to believe. Luke quotes Peter in Acts 3:16 as he explains the healing of the lame man at the Beautiful Gate: "On the basis of faith in His name, it is the name of Jesus which has strengthened this man whom you see and know." Christ is the healer, but the benefit of healing must be appropriated by faith.

It was not a magical formula quoted by Peter which brought instant health to this seriously handicapped man. No, the man himself believed in the ability and readiness of the Lord Jesus Christ to heal him.

The British scholar F. F. Bruce captures the essence of the crippled man's act of faith.

> It is through His name—the name of the once humbled and now glorified Servant of God—that this man had been cured, said Peter; and it is by faith in that same name that he has appropriated the blessing and strength which he now exhibits. The complete cure that had been accomplished was plain for all to see; Peter impressed upon them that the power that wrought the cure resided in Jesus' name, and that the man had availed himself of this power by the exercise of faith. There was no mere magical efficacy in the sounds which Peter pronounced when he commanded the cripple to walk in Jesus' name; the cripple would have known no benefit had he not responded in faith to what Peter said; but once the response was made, the power of the risen Christ filled his body with health and strength.[1]

The miracle at the Beautiful Gate was more than a demonstration of apostolic authority. Peter gives the reader no reason to believe that the lame would have been healed without exercising faith. His personal faith was necessary.

"Faith is the assurance of things hoped for. . . ." (Heb. 11:1). *Hope,* in the biblical sense, means a reasonable expectation. The lame man by the instrumentality of Peter's words regarding Christ's name was given a ground for hope. Faith was born as he laid hold of that hope which rested on the power of Jesus Christ.

Jesus Christ is the Healer. Any physical touch must be His divine work. The Word of God sets this truth before believers as a reasonable expectation.

Those who seek healing need a correct understanding of the nature of faith. It is certainly the deep assurance that the promise will be realized because of the integrity, perfection, and power of God almighty who makes the promise. But faith is more than assurance, it is obedience. The failure to comprehend this truth robs many Christians of the fruit of faith. True faith calls for a total commitment to the will of Christ.

The exercise of faith finally must be a comprehension of the triumph of Christ through His death and resurrection. The lame man believed the crucified and risen Christ for his healing. Since the atonement is the procuring cause of every redemptive benefit, faith in the efficacy of that atonement is essential to realized blessing.

The test of true faith

The gospel record of the healing of the Syrophoenician woman's daughter provides in graphic manner the concept of healing as the privilege of the believer, as was discussed in chapter one. It also enlarges on the relationship of the faith factor to healing.

> *And from there He arose and went away to the region*

of Tyre. And when He had entered a house, He wanted no one to know of it; yet He could not escape notice. But after hearing of Him, a woman whose little daughter had an unclean spirit, immediately came and fell at His feet. Now the woman was a Gentile, of the Syrophoenician race. And she kept asking Him to cast the demon out of her daughter. And He was saying to her, "Let the children be satisfied first, for it is not good to take the children's bread and throw it to the dogs." But she answered and said to Him, "Yes, Lord, but even the dogs under the table feed on the children's crumbs." And He said to her, "Because of this answer go your way; the demon has gone out of your daughter." And going back to her home, she found the child lying on the bed, the demon having departed (Mark 7:24-30).

Every exchange between the Gentile woman and Christ opened up a new door of hope for her. All the delays which tested her faith proved to be instructive. Faith is built on truth. Fantasy may produce magic, but only fact can produce a miracle. She reacted to every word Christ spoke with mounting faith that the healing she sought for her daughter would be granted.

In the second exchange Christ encouraged her by saying, "Let the children be satisfied first." The word *first* brought new hope to the woman's heart. The love and concern of the Savior for this Gentile woman and her possessed daughter were now obvious to her. She understood Him to mean that the Jews were to be first recipients of His healing touch, and then the Gentiles could hope for His mercy.

Christ gave her a second ray of hope in the statement, "It is not good to take the children's bread and throw it to the dogs." Most English versions fail to convey that by "dog" Christ meant a small household pet. The house dog was an object of its master's affection, but the master of the house would first give bread to his children before feeding his pet. With remarkable understanding and brilliant faith the woman responded, "Yes, Lord, but even the dogs under the table feed on the children's crumbs." The one who suffers and who desires his own healing may consider this answer as revealing very little faith when quite the opposite is true. The woman recognized in the words of Christ her ground for hope.

The expression *great faith* should be examined more carefully to learn its true meaning. It was the quality, not the quantity, of her faith which impressed Jesus. Much of the significance of this account has been lost by casting the conversation between Christ and the Syrophoenician woman as a conflict.

While it is true that Christ tested her faith, He did so with the intention of encouraging her. The Lord Jesus was delighted with the high level of her faith from the very start of the conversation. The testing procedure brought the bud of her faith to full bloom.

The testing of faith often takes time and requires persistence. The Scriptures set forth the propositional truths God has been pleased to disclose regarding the giving of His healing touch. These definitive statements of Scripture make up the proper ground for faith. Modern believers are often hindered in exercising faith by inadequate Bible knowledge. The Scriptures provide the seeds of faith. Time given to study, meditation, and prayer will promote the germination of those seeds of faith.

By searching the Word the believer's expectations are made consistent with what God has actually promised. E. D. Whiteside, the successful founder and pastor of Northside Alliance Church in Pittsburgh, followed the practice of refusing to anoint for healing any who did not have a definite scriptural base for faith. He would inquire of each individual the passage on which their hope of healing rested. To fix one's faith on testimonies of other people's experiences could lead to fantasy rather than faith. "So faith comes from hearing, and hearing by the word of Christ" (Rom. 10:17).

The obstacle to faith—sin

Faith has its obstacles to overcome. It is always short-circuited by sin. The toleration of known sin in a believer's life prevents faith. On the other hand faith flourishes in a clean heart.

Physical infirmity often springs from sins of the flesh and spirit which lie unconfessed in the heart. The Old Testament Scriptures name at least seven sins for which the retribution was sickness. The recognition and repentance of these sins brought deliverance while persistence in those sins brought physical death.

Miriam, the sister of Moses, was a woman of unusual leadership ability, as is illustrated by the brief biographical sketches of her in the Bible. Her career is marred by an outbreak of jealousy during the wilderness journey of the children of Israel. She, with her brother Aaron, became jealous of the leadership of Moses and proceeded to rebel at his authority. An immediate rebuke came from the Lord. Miriam stood before the camp a leper and had to be expelled from the camp because of her uncleanness.

Moses was moved with mercy and gave himself to intense intercessory prayer for her recovery. God heard his prayer and healed Miriam completely and instantaneously. Moses was so bold as to ask God to heal her immediately, but it is not always proper to ask God to heal "now." Still there are those times when impelled by the Spirit, effective prayer is made for immediate healing and, as in the case of Miriam, healing comes without delay.

In at least three other instances during Israel's wilderness experience, God visited the camp with judgment in the form of sickness. In Korah's day, there was rebellion.

God hates rebellion for it lies at the root of all sin. A rebellious attitude of heart can be the cause of sickness now as it was in Korah's day (Num. 16:40-50).

The sin of adultery brought a plague of sickness on God's people. Sexual sins disturb the whole personality. Such behavior patterns produce their own retribution often in the form of disease and crippling infirmity (Num. 25:1-9).

Israel also suffered physically as a result of widespread discontent over living conditions in the wilderness. God visited the people with judgment because of their complaints. Such an attitude of heart even in the twentieth century will sap physical vitality and encourage sickness (Num. 21:4-9).

The Bible speaks plainly of sickness that may come from over-indulgence. "On the day of our king the princes became sick with the heat of wine" (Hos. 7:5). Drunkenness produces health problems. Isaiah spoke of Ephraim as a "fading flower" due to his heavy drinking. Gluttony is equated with drunkenness as a cause of sickness. Paul referred to some men as "enemies of the cross . . . whose god is their appetite" (Phil. 3:18-19). Solomon classed the glutton with the drunkard and saw them falling equally under the judgment of God.

> *Do not be heavy drinkers of wine,*
> *Or with gluttonous eaters of meat;*
> *For the heavy drinker and the glutton will come to*
> *poverty* (Prov. 23:20-21).

It is plain that the inordinate appetites of the children of Israel brought chastening from God (Num. 11:1-6).

Healing as a blessing is never to be disassociated from Christ. The Scriptures call for a relationship to Christ who is the Great Physician. This was Simpson's reason for encouraging the believer to deliberately appropriate Christ the Healer. The relationship takes precedence over the blessing. Most of the mysteries of divine healing are resolved in understanding one's relationship to the Healer. An open, wholesome, submissive, and trusting walk with Jesus Christ takes in health and healing. Under these circumstances there is no dichotomy between the true believer's spiritual condition and his physical condition.

The obstacle to faith—Satan

A second obstacle to faith comes from Satan. His clever devices and strategies are designed to undermine faith and to create hopelessness. Often when a Christian seeks healing from Christ by faith he will experience Satan's attacks. The believer must avail himself of the whole armor of God at this point. Paul included among the pieces of that armor the "shield of faith." Satan must be resisted on the terms of Christ's victory on Calvary. The best strength a Christian can muster is not enough for battle with Satan. Only the victory of Christ can defeat the enemy.

A sick person is especially vulnerable to Satan's attacks. Depression, fear, and hopelessness press in on the mind and soul of the one who suffers physically. Self-pity overwhelms the mind, making it difficult to be objective. The emotions behave in an unpredictable pattern. Satan is not beyond taking advantage of such human weakness. God does not abandon us to the enemy's devices but provides blessed victory. The attitude of victory is the climate in which faith can take root. Fear and depression kill faith.

The Lord Jesus Christ has defeated Satan. The authority of Jesus Christ is absolute. Christ is our champion against the foe. The faith that reaches out for healing must first reach out for release from Satan's devices. The heart thus freed can soar to new heights of faith.

The obstacle to faith—misconceptions

The mystical and devotional writings of the past have too often encouraged Christians to embrace rather than to resist sickness. Unfortunately, sickness has been described in the literature of the church as an angel of mercy. Does the Bible really teach that? Sickness is an enemy to be resisted rather than welcomed as an angel. It is true that God permits sickness in the experience of His children and that if their response is appropriate, He will use the sickness as chastening to promote a better spiritual life. But never does God's Word name sickness as a blessing. It is a *curse*. An *infirmity*. Sickness is a *weakness*. An *affliction*. A *bondage*. An *enemy*. It has the smell of death. To resist sickness is both natural and spiritual.

Since healing is a part of the "children's bread" it can be assumed that healing is generally available to God's people. The limitations suggested by Scripture are few, but they are so important that all who seek healing should understand them. A. B. Simpson urged the importance of limitations.

> Any limitations there may be of healing are also fixed by certain principles; and it must be remembered that it is not immortal life that is promised in connection with the healing of the mortal body. It is sometimes asked: why should people ever die, if Christ will always heal? Because faith can only go as far as God's promise, and God has nowhere promised that we should never die during this dispensation. The prom-

ise is fulness of life, and health, and strength up to the measure of our natural life, and until our life work is done.[2]

The proper exercise of faith must consider the possible limitations to healing. The promises of God set the parameters of faith. To claim what is not set forth in propositional form by Scripture is not faith but presumption.

In addition to the limitations suggested by Dr. Simpson the sovereignty of God should be included. God can do anything that He wills. He does not always disclose to man the reasons for His actions. It is a fundamental principle that divine sovereignty supersedes human faith. There sometimes comes a point in the quest for healing where the results must be unconditionally committed to God.

The receiving hand of faith

It is significant that when Jesus was in Nazareth, His home town, He marveled at their lack of faith. The unbelief of the villagers limited Christ's work of power while in their midst. Christ has so ordered the spiritual law of receiving blessings as to require faith. Faith is the hand reached out to accept God's blessing.

Faith and prayer are coupled together in the process of receiving divine blessing. "And everything you ask in prayer, believing, you shall receive" (Matt. 21:22). This passage constitutes the laws which govern the receiving of things from God. The blessings are to them that ask. Asking is a high level of prayer. Asking is also a process of faith. This process calls for perception, patience, and perseverance. The real nature of active faith is quite different from the popular concept of faith. Dr. Simpson made the wise conclusion that faith had its instants and its hours. Prayer and faith join to seek healing with the promise of God as the only ground of appeal. With a clear understanding of the possibilities of faith the seeker keeps on asking until the answer comes.

Faith for physical healing should not be isolated from faith for other divine blessings. The Christian life is a life of faith. It calls for the understanding and development of faith. "And without faith it is impossible to please Him, for he who comes to God must believe that He is, and that He is a rewarder of those who seek Him" (Heb. 11:6). It is not a matter of just trusting God for healing, it is trusting God for everything. To receive healing by faith does not seem strange to those who walk by faith.

---

[1]F. F. Bruce, *Commentary on the Book of Acts,* p. 89.

[2]A. B. Simpson, *The Gospel of Healing,* p. 47.

12

Divine Healing in
the Ancient Church

AN UNPRECEDENTED interest in divine healing took root in Europe in the last half of the nineteenth century. As the movement spread into America at the turn of the century, it crossed many denominational lines. Though antagonists have created the impression that this was a twentieth-century innovation of sectarian interest, such thought cannot be sustained by serious theological research.

A valid study of the doctrine of healing should not only review the teaching and practice of healing in the early church as found in the book of Acts, but should also examine the teaching ministry of the Holy Spirit through the Word in all subsequent periods of church history.

A contemporary theologian provides this fitting exhortation:

> If Christ has founded a church and given it his word; if the Holy Spirit is the Teacher of the faithful; if the church is "the house of God . . . the pillar and ground of the truth" (I Tim. 3:15); then every generation of Christian theologians

must be prepared to take seriously the history of theology (broadly interpreted to include symbols, councils, theologians, treatises) as possessing manifestations of the teaching ministry of the Holy Spirit.[1]

The Ante-Nicene Church

The council of Nicea (A.D. 325) became a landmark in the development of the confessing Christian church when it established the doctrine of Christ's divinity against Arian heresy. The period from the close of the New Testament canon to the Nicean council forms an extremely important transition in the life of the church. Between A.D. 95 and 315, at least thirty-six church fathers record incidents of healing that reflect both doctrine and practice. The impressive body of literature produced by these fathers reveal insights that penetrate most of today's theological problems.

Evelyn Frost of King's College, London, wrote regarding the liturgies of this period.

> A still more valuable, although small, source of evidence found within this literature is the remains of early liturgy. There is not much that can be dated prior to Nicaea, but such as there is provides very strong and reliable evidence, for it was not composed primarily for the eyes of the world Christian, pagan, or imperial; it was composed for the worship of God. Here, then, more than in any other part of the literature except the New Testament itself, the veil is lifted upon the audience chamber in which the church is in intimate converse with her risen Lord. . . . In the heart of the converse is found much that concerns the welfare of the physical body, its healing and restoration, its preservation and its eternal welfare; the church recognized that such matters were of real importance to Him who Himself was incarnate.[2]

The apologetic and catechetical writings of the Fathers give rich insights as to how the Ante-Nicene Church understood divine healing. There are three principal doctrinal issues which emerge in these ancient treatments of divine healing. The Church Fathers associated the phenomena of physical healing with the doctrine of the resurrection. That Christ should through His name heal sick bodies was reasonable in light of the resurrection of the body. They believed the physical body was redeemed and could expect to know the benefit of redemption in some degree before the ultimate glorification of the body.

The Fathers related healing to the atonement. Justin Martyr referred to Isaiah 53:5 "through whose stripes we are healed."[3] The display of power in actual incidents of healing was attributed to Christ's death and resurrection. Their treatment of the Lord's Supper often relates healing to the Death of Christ.

The Ante-Nicene Fathers believed that the physical body of a Christian enjoyed an infusion of spiritual life just as did his spiritual nature. The doctrine of the quickening of the physical body by the Holy Spirit can be found in several writings of this period. Writing before A.D. 180, Irenaeus in *Against Heresy* refers to Paul's statement that the body is for the Lord and the Lord for the body. The body is capable of quickening and such quickening is normal for one who has life in Christ.

> But if the present temporal life, which is of such an inferior nature to eternal life, can nevertheless effect so much as to quicken our mortal members, why should not eternal life, being much more powerful than this, vivify the flesh, which has already held converse with and been accustomed to sustain life?[4]

The doctrine of healing was more than a dogma handed down from the apostles. The writings of the first three centuries indicate that the practice of the ministry of healing continued after the apostles. The cure of the sick and the exorcism of demons was well known to the public. These miracles did much to attract men to Christ.

Irenaeus verifies the widespread incidents of healing known to him:

> Those who are in truth His disciples, receiving grace from Him, do in His name perform miracles, so as to promote the welfare of other men, according to the gift which each has received from Him. For some do certainly and truly drive out devils, so that those who have been cleansed from evil spirits frequently both believe in Christ and join themselves to the church—others still, heal the sick by laying their hands upon them, and they are made whole. Yea, moreover, as I have said, the dead even have been raised up, and remained among us for many years. And what shall I more say? It is not possible to name the number of gifts which the church, scattered throughout the whole world, has received from God, in the name of Jesus Christ—and which she exerts day by day for the benefit of the Gentiles, neither practicing deception upon any, nor taking any reward from them. For as she has received freely from God, freely also she does minister (to others).[5]

The following passage from Origen, written in the third century, testifies to the frequency and effect of healing in the writer's own time:

> We assert that the whole habitable world contains evidence of the works of Jesus, in the existence of those churches of God which have been founded through Him by those who have been converted from the practice of innumerable sins. And the name of Jesus can still remove distractions from the minds of men, and expel demons, and also take away diseases.[6]

Justin Martyr in his *Apology II—To The Senate* recommends the Lord Jesus Christ because of the significant and widespread cases of healing and deliverance. He describes these cases as incurables. But in the name of Jesus healing was effected.[7]

In another discourse Justin Martyr tells Trypho that those becoming disciples of the Lord Jesus Christ received gifts from Him. He lists healing as one of those gifts.[8]

In his *Second Apology* he points out the healing office of Christ:

> Next to God, we worship and love the Word who is from the Unbegotten and ineffable God, since also He became man for our sakes, that, becoming a partaker of our sufferings, He might also bring us healing.[9]

Tertullian records the healing of the Emperor Severus after anointing by Proculus. His writings contain numerous testimonies of people from all levels of Society healed by prayer in the name of Jesus.[10]

The unction of the early church

Special attention must be given the sacrament of unction as understood by the ancient church. The shadow of its former prominence lives on in the Roman Catholic sacrament of extreme unction. The Roman Church, at about the seventh or eighth century, began the adaptation of the ordinance of anointing and eventually altered it to such extent as to change its primitive meaning entirely. Historical evidence gathered from the writings of the Fathers and the liturgies of the early church sustains the claim that for at least eight centuries after Pentecost the healing of the body was considered by the organized church a matter of faith. The writings of the church fathers contain numerous references to the practice of anointing with oil accompanied by prayer for the recovery of the sick.

Charles Wheatly, in a popular treatment of the Anglican Book of Common Prayer, deals extensively with the anointing of the sick. Of his research in the ancient writers he says,

> Accordingly, if we search into the ancient writers of the

church, we shall never find any mention of anointing, but when it was used as a rite of the gift of healing. As the gift of healing was frequent for several ages after the apostles; so we grant that the unction was often made use of to denote the miraculousness of the cure.[11]

Wheatly further concludes that the unction for healing enjoyed a renewal in the church during the seventh century.

About the seventh century, it is true, the anointing of all sick persons whatsoever began to take place; the chief enducement to which seems to have been the observation of those cures that were wrought by such as had the gift of healing.[12]

Origen deals with the passage in James, the fifth chapter, in his second homily, which authorities believe he preached about A.D. 241. Chrysostom, in a work on the authority of the priesthood, quoted James 5:13-16 and included it among those practices performed by the ministry in his day.

Cyril of Alexandria, between 412 and 428, wrote a book entitled *Worshipping in Spirit and Truth,* which makes reference to anointing and prayer for healing. He quotes the entire passage from James in a discourse on the importance of Christians avoiding the use of sorcery and magic in the recovery of illness. Cyril urges the sick to renounce sorcery, look to God, and call for anointing according to the Scriptures.

Pope Innocent I, in a letter dated March 13, 416, explained to one of his bishops that the anointing with oil described by James was a privilege that "sick faithful" had a right to expect. It is clear from the letter that the Pope understood the passage as having to do with physical healing. While Pope Innocent taught that the oil should be consecrated by the bishop, it could be administered by any Christian. He says,

> It is lawful not for the priests only, but for all Christians to
> use the oil in their own need or in the needs of the members
> of their household.[13]

Among the notable references to anointing for health
in the writings of the church fathers, are two sermons written by Caesarius of Arles who presided over that See from
502 to 542. It would appear that the members of his parish
were especially tempted to resort to spiritualists for physical healing. To counteract the danger of such a practice
Caesarius taught the true means of divine healing found in
the New Testament.

Caesarius in a sermon urged the faithful, in the event of
sickness, to turn to the church rather than to demonism
for healing.

> As often as any sickness comes on anyone, let him who is
> sick receive the Body and Blood of Christ, and then let him
> anoint his own body; so that that which is written may be
> fulfilled in him. "Is anyone sick, let him call for the presby-
> ters of the church; and let them pray over him anointing
> him with oil in the Name of the Lord: and then prayer of
> faith will save him that is sick, and the Lord shall raise him
> up. . . ." You see, brethren, that he, who is in sickness,
> should run to the church and he will merit to receive health
> of body and to receive pardon of his sins. Since therefore
> two good things can be got in the church, why do miserable
> men strive to bring on themselves multiplied evils by resort-
> ing to fountains, trees, and diabolical phylacteries and the
> branding of magical marks on their body and by consulting
> diviners and soothsayers and fortune tellers?[14]

Any consideration of the Church Fathers on the subject
of anointing ought not to overlook Bede who wrote a commentary on the book of James between A.D. 709 and 716.
He clearly testifies to the use of anointing in the Church of
England in his own time and that remarkable healings had
occurred as a result of this practice. Bede wrote,

"And let them pray over him, anointing him. . . ." We read in the Gospel that the apostles also did this; and at the present time it remains the custom of the church, that the sick should be anointed by the presbyters with consecrated oil, and that anointing being accompanied by prayer, they should be restored to health.[15]

Two church councils during the ninth century produced canon on the unction for physical healing. The first of these was Council-sur-Saone held in 813. The forty-eighth canon of this council urges the practice of anointing according to James not be taken lightly. Local elders were permitted to anoint with oil consecrated by the bishop. The Council of Pavier held as late as 850 presented to the church a canon with instructions on the anointing with oil for the restoration of bodily health.

It would appear from these canons that the change of the unction from an ordinance for physical healing to a sacrament designed to prepare believers for death did not make serious inroads into the thinking of the church before the ninth century.

Perhaps the most complete scholarly work written in modern times on the rite of anointing is *The Anointing of the Sick* by Rev. F. W. Puller. The book is made up of four lectures delivered in 1903 to the Westminster House of the Society of Saint John the Evangelist. A renewed interest in anointing as practiced in primitive times had emerged in the Church of England. Puller's treatment is helpful both from the exposition he gives of James 5 and the extensive research on the history of healing in the established church.

Puller draws some conclusions from his research which he summarized in the following words:

I think I have shown that from the time of the Apostles onwards, during the first seven centuries of our era, the custom of praying over sick people and anointing them with holy oil continued without any break. And there seems to me to be good reasons for believing that in many cases the petitions that were offered were granted, and that the holy oil was used by God as a channel for conveying health to the sick persons. And I have never been able to understand the theory which admits supernatural cures in the apostolic age, but denies the truth of all similar cures in later ages. Certainly the church was unconscious of any such idea.[16]

The transition of the sacrament of anointing from a ritual for healing to one of penance was a gradual one in both the Western and the Eastern church. There seems to be some historical evidence that the change in the church's view of penance from the seventh century had a bearing on the alteration of the purpose of anointing. Penance in the earlier centuries had been applicable only to those Christians conscious of some very deadly sin in their lives. By the eighth century the doctrine of penance was being widely applied to all Christians.

It may have been this doctrinal change which influenced churchmen to interpret the conditional clause in James 5 as applying to every sick person. This explanation seems to be a plausible theory for the change regarding the function of anointing from bodily health to that of the Roman church doctrine of extreme unction.

After centuries of limiting the rite of anointing to the use of extreme unction, the Roman Church revised its position at the Second Vatican Council. The provisional text for the new rite published by the bishops on the liturgy explains the "unction" as intended for the restoration of the sick.

The Second Vatican Council adds the following:

Extreme Unction, which may also be more fittingly called "anointing of the sick," is not a sacrament for those only who are at the point of death.[17]

The decree on anointing explains the relationship of the rite to physical healing.

> When the church cares for the sick, it serves Christ Himself in the suffering members of His mystical body. When it follows the example of the Lord Jesus, who "went about doing good and healing" (Acts 10:38), the church obeys his command to cure the sick. (See Mark 16:18).
>
> The church shows this solicitude not only by visiting those who are in poor health but also by raising them up through the sacrament of anointing and by nourishing them with the eucharist during their illness and in danger of death.[18]

The provisional text allows the anointing of the sick in large numbers at gatherings in the church, or the larger gatherings of a parish or diocese. The Roman Church has made a complete circle in its interpretation of anointing and has recently returned to that position which was common to the whole church until the eighth century.

From a theological viewpoint the prayers and liturgies of the first eight centuries of the church supply strong evidence that the practice of healing was part of the church life, not just an isolated incident here and there. The healing of the sick seems to have had a place in the regular ministry of the church.

The liturgy of St. Mark is an example. In this instance the prayer for healing, as Peder Olsen points out, has a natural and organic place in the liturgy.

> Graciously look to us O Lord, and heal the sick among your people. Deliver them and us, O Lord, from all illness and expel from us the spirit of weakness. O Lord, Healer of both body and soul, thou who carest for all flesh, look upon us and heal us by thy saving power from all illness, both of the body and soul. Deliver the captives, heal the sick.[19]

The theological implication of this prayer is significant. Interest in the language of prayer is a dogma of physical healing. The recovery of the sick is here presented as the privilege of the believer. "Heal the sick among your people." The petition suggests that physical healing was redemption related: "Heal us with thy *saving power.*"

About the turn of the century the Sacramentary of Saint Serapion was discovered. Serapion, who lived during the fourth century, was a resident of Tumeris on the Nile Delta. Tradition says he was a friend of Athanasius. The following prayer from Serapion's Sacramentary was offered for the consecration of oil for anointing the sick:

> We invoke Thee who hast all authority and power, the Savior of all men, Father of our Lord Jesus Christ, and we pray thee to send out a healing power of the only begotten from heaven upon this oil, that it may become to those who are being anointed with it for a throwing off of every disease and every infirmity, for a prophylactic against every demon, for a separation of every unclean spirit, for an expulsion of every evil spirit, for a driving out of all fever and shivering fits and every infirmity, for a medicine of life and recovery, for health and soundness in all their parts of soul, body, spirit, for perfect strengthening. O Master, let every Satanic operation, every demon, every snare of the adversary, every plague, every scourge, every smart, every pain, or stroke, or shaking, or evil shadow, fear Thy Holy Name which we have now invoked, and the Name of the Only-Begotten; and let them depart from the inward and outward parts of these Thy servants, that His name may be glorified, who for us was crucified and rose again, who took up our sicknesses and our infirmities, even Jesus Christ, and who is coming to judge quick and dead. Because through Him to Thee are the glory and strength both now and to all ages of the ages. Amen.[20]

The priestly consecration of the oil cannot be commended, but the content of the prayer offers rare insight into the thinking of the times, especially the explicit implication of the interpretation of Matthew 8:17: "Who took up our sicknesses and our infirmities, even Jesus Christ."

These samplings from the writings of the ancient church demonstrate that they anointed the sick with oil expecting recovery. The combination of spiritual decline and sacerdotalism gradually reduced the effectiveness of anointing with oil. The church accommodated itself to the reality by giving this practice of anointing an entirely different meaning. The rite was no longer intended to be therapeutic but preparatory for death.

---

[1] Bernard Ramm, *The Pattern of Authority*, p. 57.

[2] Evelyn Frost, *Christian Healing*, p. 121.

[3] Alexander Roberts and James Donaldson, eds., *The Ante-Nicene Fathers*, 1:87.

[4] *Ibid.*, 1:529.

[5] *Ibid.*, 1:539.

[6] *Ibid.*, 4:426-7.

[7] *Ibid.*, 1:193.

[8] *Ibid.*, 1:214.

[9] *Ibid.*, 1:192-93.

[10] *Ibid.*, 2:690-91.

[11] Charles Wheatly, *A Rational Illustration of the Book of Common Prayer*, p. 443.

[12] *Ibid.*, p. 444.

[13] F. W. Puller, *Anointing of the Sick*, pp. 67-68.

[14] *Ibid.*

[15] *Ibid.*, p. 48.

[16] *Ibid.*, pp. 188-89.

[17] *Rite of Anointing and Pastoral Care of the Sick*, p. 7.

[18] *Ibid.*, p. 3.

[19] Peder Olsen, *Healing Through Prayer*, p. 12.

[20] W. F. Puller, *Anointing of the Sick*, pp. 88-89.
Serapion's Sacramentary, Rubric: *A Prayer for Oil for the Sick or for Bread or for Water*, translated from the Greek by W. F. Puller from a text which dates to the eleventh century.

13

The Modern
Healing Movement

THE DECLINE IN HEALING dates from the ninth century, but the ministry never ceased entirely even during the
Middle Ages. With the quickening of the church even in
pre-Reformation days a new interest in anointing for healing was evident.

Pre-Reformation

The documents of the Middle Ages are not as reliable as
those of the ancient church. It must be admitted that many
of the healing claims from this period are spurious. Magic
and witchcraft abounded in Europe, with the result that
mediumistic healing became confused with the healing of
the church.

There were some reliable accounts of healing during the
Middle Ages. Bernard of Clairvaux (1091-1153) believed

that Christ was still able to heal the sick in his day. Many came to Bernard for prayer, with remarkable results. No doubt the purest practice of healing during this period was to be found among the Waldensians. An examination of the Waldensian Christians of the Piedmont, a remote mountain area in the Alps Mountains, throws light on the historical aspect of the practice of anointing. The history of these stalwart saints has challenged most serious-minded Christians for many generations. The origin of their form of Christianity cannot be documented, but the evidence points toward the apostolic period. Hidden in their mountain stronghold, they were preserved from the errors of the Romish Church. In isolation they continued to practice that which had been given them "in the beginning."

Beza, Calvin's successor, said of the Waldensian church that they were the seed of the pure Christian church— "being those who had been appointed by the wonderful providence of God, whom none of the storms by which the world had been shaken, nor persecution, have been able to prevail or to yield a voluntary submission to Roman tyranny and idolatry." The doctrine held by these simple Christians was that same pure strain of apostolic truth uncovered at great price by the Reformers.

The Waldensians had not been influenced by those forces which altered the teaching of anointing with oil. They knew nothing of the doctrine of extreme unction. In 1431 the Waldensian Confession said this of anointing for physical healing:

> "Therefore, concerning this anointing of the sick, we hold it *as an article of faith,* and profess sincerely from the heart that sick persons, when they ask it, may lawfully be anointed with the anointing oil by one who joins with them in praying that it may be efficacious to the healing of the body according to the design and end and effect mentioned by the apostles."[1]

The Reformation period

The reformation in the English church did not overlook the correction of the Roman interpretation of the unction. The Bishop's Book published in 1537 in defense of the Reformation deals at length with the doctrine of unction and its abuses. It clearly makes unction a matter of physical healing:

> The grace conferred in this Sacrament is the relief and recovery of the disease and sickness wherewith the sick is then diseased and troubled, and also the remission of his sins if he be then in sin.[2]

The first Book of Common Prayer compiled by the English Church after its break with Rome was known as the Prayer Book of King Edward VI. At the close of the office for the Visitation of the Sick is found a liturgy for the anointing service. The prayer contained in this liturgy shows the extent to which the English church had reformed the sacrament of unction:

> As with visible oil this body outwardly is anointed, so our Heavenly Father, Almighty God, grant of his infinite goodness, that thy soul inwardly may be anointed with the Holy Ghost, who is the Spirit of all strength, comfort, relief, and gladness. And vouchsafe for his great mercy (if it be his blessed will) to restore unto thee thy bodily health and strength to serve him; and send the release of all thy pains, troubles, and diseases, both in mind and body.[3]

The English church during its reformation abandoned the Roman doctrine of extreme unction and returned to what the Reformers believed to be apostolic: anointing for physical healing.

The great German reformer, Martin Luther, also came to grips with this doctrine. He personally had a strong faith in divine healing. He encouraged prayer for the sick and practiced it in his own life. The record shows that on at least three occasions Luther prayed for the seriously ill and saw remarkable healing. Both Luther's wife, Katherine, and his coworker, Melanchthon, were saved from death by God's healing touch in answer to prayer. Peder Olsen, a Norwegian Lutheran scholar, says of Luther's position on unction:

> Luther also had a statement in 1529 about James 5:14-15 and anointing with oil in the name of the Lord. He permits anointing on the condition that this act not be made into a sacrament.[4]

A. J. Gordon says of Luther's view of divine healing:

> He believed in and spoke with all the vehemence of his Saxon heart on the side of present miracles.[5]

He then quotes Luther on the subject of supernatural healing:

> How often has it happened and still does, that devils have been driven out in the name of Christ, also by calling on his name and prayer that the sick have been healed?[6]

Post-Reformation period

At the beginning of the eighteenth century the Anabaptists were making an impact upon the religious life of Europe and Germany in particular. The Reformation churches were by this time so involved with the state that many sincere believers were seeking a purification of the church. This grass roots movement, while at times plagued by excessive mysticism, was nevertheless able to make a significant contribution to the recovery of apostolic Christianity. Small cells of believers gathered in homes for the purpose of Bible study. The leadership for the most part was composed of laymen.

The Anabaptists stand out in the long history of the Free

Church Movement. They restored a simplicity of worship akin to that found in the primitive church. The Bible was their only rule of faith and practice. Their concepts of church order were taken strictly from the New Testament. Many of the Anabaptists revived the practice of anointing the sick with oil.

Alexander Mack of Swartznau, Germany, led out a small group of believers in 1708 to establish a church built on New Testament principles. The movement has been known in subsequent church history as "The Dunker Church" because of their practice of triune immersion. Mack and his followers, pressured by persecution, migrated to America early in the eighteenth century. The movement today consists of four major groups, all founded largely in America: the Old Order German Baptist Brethren, the Church of the Brethren, the Brethren Church, and the Grace Brethren Church. All four groups continue to teach and practice the anointing of the sick in accordance with James 5. The literature of the movement records many testimonies of miraculous recoveries in answer to prayers of faith.

A contemporary of Alexander Mack, Menno Simons, founder of the various Mennonite branches, came to a similar understanding of the Scriptures. The Mennonites, like the Dunkers, were also a part of the Anabaptist movement. They, too, came to the practice of anointing as a result of inductive study of the Scripture, and many Mennonite groups still anoint and pray for the sick after the pattern laid down by the apostle James.

The healing movement in Europe

The revival of divine healing in modern times seems to have its beginnings on the continent of Europe. Revival visited many parts of Germany early in the nineteenth century. While this resurgence of spiritual life came in the institutional church, the movement had many of the marks of apostolic Christianity. Some historians have described it as something of a new pietism.

The evangelist of this period looked for a recovery of biblical charismatic gifts. It was not uncommon in the movement for the sick to be healed and demons cast out. The voices of this new movement were often spiritual leaders of great stature in the church.

It is the name of Johannes Christopher Blumhardt that is most frequently associated with the ministry of divine healing during that period. Blumhardt pastored a congregation at Mottlingen in the Black Forest of south Germany. One of his parishioners had become possessed with demons. Blumhardt, concerned for this case, set himself to pray for her complete deliverance, the struggle lasting for a full two years. At last by prayer, fasting, and claiming the merits of Jesus' name the demon was exorcised. The experience left a deep impression upon Pastor Blumhardt and his church. The aftermath of this remarkable deliverance was a communitywide spiritual awakening. The revival penetrated much of the Black Forest area and was accompanied by deep repentance and many lasting conversions.

Eventually Blumhardt became burdened with the pressures of serving his parish and at the same time ministering to the many sufferers who came to him from all parts of Germany. After waiting upon the Lord a solution to the problem came about. A very spacious home had been constructed at Bad Boll to accommodate visitors coming from sulphur baths located in that region. This business venture failed and the property became available to Blumhardt. In a remarkable way the funds were provided. Pastor Blumhardt resigned the Mottlingen parish and set to work establishing a home of instruction and prayer for the mentally and spiritually sick. The Lord's hand of blessing was upon this move. Bad Boll became the pattern for many such centers for spiritual refreshing and bodily healing. These "Houses of Blessing" were found not only in Europe, but also in America the pattern of ministry was adopted by some. The popularity of such rest homes continued until after World War I. Otto Stockmayer, Johannes Seitz, Pastor Bohmerle, and other outstanding German evangelists opened homes similar to Bad Boll.

The philosophy of the Bible rest home was quite simple. Blumhardt was of the conviction that seekers needed instruction and time to lay hold of God's provision for healing. The rest home provided a peaceful atmosphere along with freedom from routine responsibilities. In this atmosphere the sufferer could meditate on the Word and search his own heart. Sound Bible teaching was given each day. The pastor also invited the residents to his office for counseling, which gave attention to their individual needs. Prayer and the laying on of hands was practiced as well.

The influence of Blumhardt still persists to the present time. His writings are kept in print and are still read by evangelicals in the state church. The most important influence from Blumhardt's ministry was in his own time. Dr. Paulus Scharpff, a German Methodist historian, believes that Blumhardt made a major contribution to the theology of his day:

> Neander, Tholuck and Blumhardt greatly influenced the theology of the nineteenth and twentieth centuries, especially the revival theology of the next hundred years.[7]

The "Gemeinschaft," an evangelical fellowship within the state church of Germany, was influenced by Blumhardt's revival emphasis. Several of Germany's greatest revivalists were men who shared Blumhardt's views. For this reason divine healing was a factor in many of the revival movements in Germany from 1860 until the early part of the nineteenth century.

No history of the healing movement of the nineteenth century should overlook Dorthea Trudel, the Swiss deaconess whose remarkable ministry with the sick became known throughout the world. The rest home she established in Mannendorf was a haven for suffering believers from many lands. Miss Trudel's ministry benefited not only those with physical maladies but also those with mental illnesses as she effectively prayed for them. Her method of instruction and prayer resembled Blumhardt's work at Bad Boll. Miss Trudel died in 1862 but the Mannendorf home continued well into the twentieth century. The godly German evangelist, Samuel Zeller, became her successor.

While the revival of the charisma of healing thrived in Germany, Switzerland, and other European countries, a similar movement emerged in Great Britain. The Bethshan Conference on the Deeper Life and Divine Healing established by W. R. Boardman in Great Britain was the bridge by which renewal came from Europe. Dr. Boardman invited Otto Stockmayer, Johannes Blumhardt, and Samuel Zeller to minister on the doctrine of healing at Bethshan. Since Dr. Boardman was an American and had many associations in the United States, he frequently invited influential clergymen from America to the Bethshan conference. Among them were Dr. Charles Cullis of Boston and Dr. A. B. Simpson of New York. Both men were greatly influenced by Boardman and by the European leaders of the healing movement. Boardman, like Blumhardt, instituted a home for spiritual ministry and physical healing at Bethshan.

Among the most famous to visit Boardman's home was

Andrew Murray of South Africa. The great Reformed pastor had arrived in London to see a specialist for treatment of a serious throat condition, which prevented him from preaching. After hearing Boardman preach on healing, Dr. Murray canceled his appointment with the doctor and, instead, registered at the home in Bethshan. God wonderfully touched Murray and restored his health. Under the instruction of Boardman and later of Stockmayer, Murray became convinced that healing was a vital truth that should be a part of the church's ministry. He authored a book on the subject and continued to preach divine healing for the remainder of his ministry.

By 1875, healing homes were flourishing in England. Deeper life conferences were called to teach physical healing as a part of the benefits of Christ's work in man's behalf. Mr. Boardman and Lord Rockstad were among the leaders of this movement.

The literature of the healing movement, along with the public conferences to propagate this truth, was the means by which the ministry of healing came to America.

Benjamin Warfield, who was generally critical of the ministry of healing, had this to say about its widespread influence by 1875:

> Already thirty years ago (1875) there were more than thirty "Faith Homes" established in America for the treatment of disease by prayer alone; and in England and on the European Continent there were many more. International Conferences had already been held by its advocates and conventions of narrower constituency beyond number. It counts adherents in every church and if for no other reason than its great diffusion it demands careful attention.[8]

Otto Stockmayer can no doubt be credited with spreading the revival of healing beyond the borders of Germany. This popular evangelist and Bible teacher made a deep impression on the evangelical community of Great Britain on his visits there. Stockmayer visited the United States and preached in many churches and conferences. It seems that England forms the link by which the renewal of physical healing eventually came to America.

Before Boardman and the influence of the Bethshan Conference, a significant healing ministry occurred in London at the Metropolitan Tabernacle pastored by Charles H. Spurgeon. The popular interest in the successful prayers of Spurgeon for the sick became so great that in 1861 he used his pulpit to put down the extravagances that were building up. Spurgeon refused to make any claims of healing power, always keeping the healing ministry in perspective.

Russel H. Conwell, Spurgeon's biographer, devoted an entire chapter to testimonies of miraculous healings in answer to Mr. Spurgeon's prayers. Conwell summarizes the healing ministry at Metropolitan Tabernacle under Spurgeon's leadership:

> For twenty-five years it has been one of the most frequent things to hear mentioned in public the request of some person who was sick, for the prayers of the church that God might send a speedy recovery. The very fact that the numbers of such applicants increased year after year, is in itself satisfactory evidence that the people who were prayed for at first must have believed that the prayers of the church were answered, and advertized the fact among their friends.
>
> Thousands of cases like those we have related might be gathered, and a great number of them have been collected, showing the wonderful agency of some Divine power exercised in prayer.[9]

Spurgeon had no elaborate theology of healing, though he occasionally preached on the subject. Much of his healing ministry took place in the course of pastoral visitation.

The healing movement in America

In America the Methodist Church was one of the first to be touched by the healing movement. Some outstanding Methodist theologians and church administrators became exponents of Christ, the Healer. Daniel Steele of Boston University was perhaps the greatest voice of Wesleyanism in his day. His books are widely read today. In a letter written to Jennie Smith, an outstanding Quaker woman who was wonderfully healed, dated June 9, 1879, Dr. Steele says,

> I am praying the Lord to heal me, with or without means, if it be His will. Ever since reading the chapter on faith-cures in Dr. Bushnell's *Nature and the Supernatural,* I have believed that the gift of healing has been in the church in all ages.[10]

Rev. Charles J. Fowler, a Methodist and president of the National Holiness Association, published a book entitled *Thoughts on Prayer*, in which he quotes one of his contemporaries, Bishop Warren of the Methodist Church, on healing:

> This interpretation makes prominent the scripture doctrine that spiritual power is conducive to physical welfare. The Bible is full of this doctrine and so is all true philosophy. . . . All the great of Christian advance have had faith to apply to God in earnest prayer for physical welfare for themselves and for others. Christ set the example in strict consonance with Old Testament practice.[11]

Fowler also quotes an important statement from John Wesley on the permanence of healing in the church:

> This single conspicuous gift (of healing) which Christ committed to his Apostles remained in the Church long after the other miraculous gifts were withdrawn. Indeed it seems to be designed to remain always, and St. James directs the elders who were the most, if not the only gifted men, to

administer it. This was the whole process of psyche in the Christian Church till it was lost through unbelief.[12]

Wesley's conclusion is worthy of consideration. Subsequent church history vindicates the position that the withdrawal of healing in the church would indicate a low spiritual condition among believers.

The teaching of divine healing spread across America through the Methodist camp meetings. That segment of Methodism which stressed the Wesleyan position of scriptural holiness also preached a very moderate and sane message of divine healing. It is for this reason that all the newer denominations born out of Methodism between 1870 and 1920 teach, and to some extent practice, anointing with oil and prayer for the sick. The following church bodies of Wesleyan persuasion can be cited: the Church of the Nazarene, the Wesleyan Methodist, the Free Methodist, Pilgrim Holiness, and the Church of God (Anderson, Indiana).

Dr. Charles Cullis, an Episcopal physician, carried on a remarkable healing ministry in Boston. His compassion for the sick led him to establish by faith a home for consumptive patients. Dr. Cullis was introduced to the doctrine of healing by Dr. W. E. Boardman. He then altered his ministry to include instruction and prayer for the sick.

The healing of Bishop Simpson in answer to prayer no doubt made an impact on Methodism. The account of his healing was published in *The Methodist Advocate* magazine and given national attention. Bishop Bowman, who wrote the account of Bishop Simpson's healing, states that ten thousand other cases of such healing in answer to prayer could be cited.[13]

William Patton made a collection of healing testimonies from this period taken largely from Methodist publications.

While the truth of healing was widely held among evangelicals of the Middle West, it also had its strong champions on the East Coast. Calvary Baptist Church in New York City enjoyed a fruitful prayer ministry for the sick. The pastor of that great church, Dr. John Roach Straton, wrote *Divine Healing in Scripture and Life*, a classic book on the subject. Dr. A. J. Gordon, another outstanding Baptist leader and founder of Gordon College and Seminary, held firmly to the scriptural doctrine of healing. The noted lay Bible teacher and conference speaker S. D. Gordon, author of the famous *Quiet Talk* Series, was also of the persuasion that the sick could be healed today in answer to prayer. He authored a sane and helpful book on the doctrine entitled *Quiet Talks About the Healing Christ.*

Baptists, Congregationalists, and others also reported healings during the last half of the nineteenth century. Rev. Charles Finney, revivalist and for many years president of Oberlin College, verified the remarkable healing of Mrs. R. D. Miller. Encouraged by reading the story of Dorthea Trudel of Mannendorf, Switzerland, Mrs. Miller began to look to God for the healing of her pain-racked body. During a prayer meeting on September 26, 1872, God instantly relieved her of her pain and she was restored to health. She was the wife of a prominent Congregational minister and the account of her healing influenced many to embrace the scriptural teaching of divine healing.

By the turn of the century, interest in the truth of divine healing ran high in evangelical circles. A sample of the general attitude of Christians toward the doctrine may be seen in the book *Getting Things from God* by Charles A. Blanchard, then president of Wheaton College. Dr. Blanchard relates numerous instances of healings in his own family and among those to whom he ministered. He advocated the practice of anointing the sick according to James 5.

Dr. Blanchard refutes the errors of Christian Science by expounding the true position of the New Testament on healing. He points out that Christian Science ignores the many testimonies of healing coming from the Bible-believing churches, and he makes the following statement about two great evangelical churches of the English-speaking world in that day:

> When Spurgeon's work was beginning in England, it was one of the commonplaces that sick people were prayed for by the elders of that great church and were recovered. No man can worship thirty days with the Moody Church in Chicago without hearing ten, scores, perhaps hundreds of prayers requested and offered for sick people, and all people familiar with the life of that great church know that God hears and answers prayers.[14]

Further testimonies of healing at Moody Church and Bible Institute may be found in a Colportage book printed in 1918. A section of twenty-three pages of testimonies is entitled "Prayer for the Recovery of the Sick."

Hearing Restored

While a pastor in Illinois, one day a sharp noise, almost like the snap of a small revolver, startled me and I found that the drum of my left ear had broken. I was sent by Dr. Boynton to one of the best ear specialists in Chicago, who would give me no hope, saying that a puncture of that size seldom healed. I made him ten visits, and he said the ear was no better except in general appearance. I had told Dr. Boynton that I wanted God to heal me and asked him to pray for me. I asked the prayers of others also. I prayed daily for several weeks for healing. After the tenth visit to the doctor I went to my room in the Moody Bible Institute and had an especially earnest time in prayer. I retired, resting my case assuringly with God. When I awoke next morning my hearing was entirely restored, seeming more acute than before.

Optic Nerves Restored

It was while at the Bible Institute (Chicago) in 1898, that I had serious trouble with the optic nerve, so that I was unable to study or read more than perhaps five minutes continuously. The retina of the eyes became so exceedingly sensitive that even the light was painful.

I was excused from all class work, and for the first time in my life began to think of calling upon God for divine healing. I had heard Dr. R. A. Torrey speak on this subject in the classroom; so I went to him and asked if he thought God would be pleased to intervene in my case. Dr. Torrey said he was sure that if I would take my stand on the promise of James 5:14-16 God would heal me.

Accordingly we arranged that at Dr. Torrey's home he would anoint me that day at noon. At the appointed hour, together with Mrs. Curtis, we went to the home of our friend. After the anointing and prayer, I went directly to my study and took up all my class work.[15]

The teaching of divine healing had attained wide acceptance in the churches of America by the turn of the century. The movement knew no denominational boundaries. Men of stature in most every segment of the evangelical community endorsed the practice of anointing.

The widespread interest in the new Christian Science movement brought the matter of supernatural healing to public attention. Theosophy was becoming popular during this same period of time. Evangelical leaders were often enlightened on the biblical position of healing by their research to refute the errors of Christian Science and theosophy.

Care must be taken in tracing the historical development of the doctrine of physical healing to distinguish the healing movement related to biblical Christianity and the movement as manifested in the cults. The cults can hardly be equated with the substantial ministry of divine healing found in the established church. The mind-over-matter cults, spiritism, fanaticism, and witchcraft are not under consideration in this study. All the groups and leaders to which the author makes reference would endorse historic Christianity. They were exponents of biblical truth. The author believes that the evidence of church history supports the premise that there is a proper doctrine of divine healing that has persisted from apostolic times until the present and is a part of historic Christian doctrine. It is not an innovation of modern times.

Most every facet of revealed truth has been counterfeited by the forces of darkness. Divine healing has been no exception. It is possible to trace the trail of false healing across the centuries. It has always been associated with the perversion of the basic doctrines of the Christian system. The founders of such movements are false prophets denying the true nature of Christ, the atonement of His blood. They abound in extra-biblical sources of revelation. The Christian does well to avoid any association with such false teachers.

Unfortunately, some writers have given the impression that the practice of healing in today's church has its roots in Pentecostalism. This is not true. The modern healing movement began a full half century before the Pentecostal movement emerged. The Pentecostal groups received their basic teachings from the historic healing movement and sometimes added their own peculiar innovations. The contemporary charismatic movement for the most part reflects the healing theology of classical Pentecostalism.

Divine healing has been quietly practiced in Protestantism from the dawn of the Reformation until now. Some evangelical denominations of Anabaptist background in the United States can trace their practice of anointing to the eighteenth century. The Anglican Church can go back to the sixteenth century reformation of the English church.

Church history proves that the renewal of the unction for healing is not a recent innovation in the church. The most significant healing movements in modern times have been non-Pentecostal. There are at least eighteen evangelical denominations in the United States which practice anointing and prayer for physical healing. All of these are non-Pentecostal movements.

A number of writers have made A. B. Simpson the founder of the modern healing movement, but the facts do not sustain this position. The doctrine of healing embraced by Simpson had been preached across Europe and Britain for two decades before he took up the teaching. Books on the subject of healing were already in print and widely read before Simpson experienced physical healing. He did not introduce any new tenets to the teaching.

Dr. Simpson's contribution was in propagating this scriptural teaching of divine healing with such skill and vigor that it made a great impact on the evangelical church in America. Leaders in many denominational churches preached divine healing with enthusiasm during the first two decades of the twentieth century.

Simpson was the focal point of most of the written attacks on divine healing because he was well known and because he succeeded in bringing the doctrine of healing to public notice. His writings on the subject have survived and are more widely read today than those of most of his contemporaries. Much of what he had to say on healing was practical and devotional. He did not produce a theological work on the subject.

The considerable interest aroused by Simpson in the doctrine of healing is evidenced by the number of lecture series and books produced by leading theological educators across America on this subject. Benjamin Warfield lectured on this issue at Columbia Theological Seminary in 1917. His interest had been stirred by an article appearing in *Century* magazine on healing, written by one of Simpson's co-workers, Kelso Carter. Charles Brown of Yale made an exhaustive study of the church's ministry of healing and authored at least two books on the subject.

The renewal of healing reached into many of the historic Reformation churches and its practice continued well into the 1930s. Eventually the excesses practiced among some Pentecostals brought many of the churches to silence on this doctrine. They feared that the teaching on healing would identify them as Pentecostal. The Christian and Missionary Alliance, along with a number of other newly formed evangelical bodies, continued to teach and practice the anointing with oil of the sick for healing. All of these church bodies drew their teaching on divine healing from the historic healing movement.

A survey of the doctrine of healing across the centuries of church history proves it to be a part of the historic Christian faith and not an innovation of the twentieth century. It further proves that the doctrine of healing has at times emerged in all the historic churches, both Protestant and Catholic. Most frequently, the ministry of healing returns to the church in times of intense spiritual renewal. Healing has not been associated with any particular system of theology. Both Calvinists and Arminians have embraced and practiced it. Churches with liturgy and those with spontaneous worship have believed this truth. The practice of healing after James 5:13-16 is far too widespread to be ignored by any serious churchman.

---

[1]Quoted by A. J. Gordon in *The Ministry of Healing,* p. 65.

[2]J. R. Pridie, *The Church's Ministry of Healing,* p. 82.

[3]Charles Wheatly, *A Rational Illustration of the Book of Common Prayer,* p. 439.

[4]Peder Olsen, *Healing Through Prayer,* p. 15.

[5]A. J. Gordon, *The Ministry of Healing,* p. 92.

[6]*Ibid.*

[7]Paulus Scharpff, *The History of Evangelism,* p. 129.

[8]Benjamin B. Warfield, *Miracles: Yesterday and Today,* p. 158.

[9]Russell H. Conwell, *Life of Charles Haddon Spurgeon,* pp. 184-85.

[10]Jennie Smith, *Baca to Beulah*, pp. 354-55.

[11]Charles J. Fowler, *Thoughts on Prayer,* pp. 108-9.

[12]*Ibid.,* pp. 91-92.

[13]D. W. LeLachuer, "Divine Healing," *Living Truths,* October 1903, pp. 195-6.

[14]Charles A. Blanchard, *Getting Things from God,* p. 214.

[15]Henry Adams, et al., eds., *I Cried, He Answered,* pp. 12-13.

Bibliography

Adams, Henry; Camp, Norman H.; Norton, William; and Stevens, F. A., eds. *I Cried, and He Answered: A Faithful Record of Remarkable Answers to Prayer.* Chicago: Bible Institute Colportage Assn., 1918. Pp. 11-23.

Alexander, Joseph A. *Commentary on the Prophecies of Isaiah.* Reprint. Grand Rapids, Mich.: Zondervan Publishing House, 1953.

Alford, Henry. *The Greek New Testament.* 6 vols. Cambridge: Deighton, Bell & Co. 1871.

Bainbridge, Harriette S. *Life for Soul and Body.* New York: Alliance Press Co., 1906.

Ballard, J. Hudson. *Spirit, Soul and Body.* New York: Alliance Press Co., 1910.

Barnes, Albert. *Notes on the Old Testament: Psalms.* Vol. 2. Reprint. Grand Rapids, Mich.: Baker Book House, 1959.

Bauman, Louis S. *The Faith Once for All Delivered unto the Saints.* Published by the author, 1947. Pp. 83-86.

Bede, Venerable. *The Ecclesiastical History of the English Nation.* Orig. ms., A.D. 731. 1st printing, 1473. Reprint. London: J. M. Dent & Co., 1903.

Biederwolf, W. E. *Whipping Post Theology.* Grand Rapids, Mich.: Wm. B. Eerdmans Publishing Co., 1934.

Bingham, Rowland. *The Bible and the Body.* Edinburgh: Marshall, Morgan, & Scott, 1952.

Blanchard, Charles A. *Getting Things from God.* Chicago: Bible Colportage Assn., 1915. Pp. 87-95, 211-18. The fourfold formula used by A. B. Simpson appears on p. 218.

Bosworth, F. F. *Christ the Healer.* Published by the author, 1924.

Brockington, A. Allen. *Old Testament Miracles in the Light of the Gospel.* Edinburgh: T. & T. Clark, 1907. Pp. 101-112.

Bruce, F. F. *Commentary on the Book of Acts.* Grand Rapids, Mich.: Wm. B. Eerdmans Publishing Co., 1971.

232

Bushnell, Horace. *Nature and the Supernatural.* New York: Charles Scribner's Sons, 1887.

Byrum, E. E. *Miracles and Healing.* Anderson, Ind.: Gospel Trumpet Co., 1919.

Carter, R. Kelso. *Faith Healing Reviewed After Twenty Years.* Chicago: Christian Witness Co., 1897.

_____. *The Atonement for Sin and Sickness.* Boston: Willard Tract Repository, 1884.

Chadwick, Samuel. *The Path of Prayer.* Kansas City, Mo.: Beacon Hill Press, 1931.

Cobb, E. Howard. *Christ Healing.* London: Marshall, Morgan & Scott, 1960.

Conwell, Russell H. *Life of Charles Haddon Spurgeon.* Philadelphia: Edgewood Publishing Co., 1892. Pp. 172-194.

Cullis, Charles. *Have Faith in God* (Dr. Cullis and His Work). Boston: Willard Tract Repository, 1885.

_____. *More Faith Cures.* Boston: Willard Tract Repository, 1881.

_____. *Other Faith Cures.* Boston: Willard Tract Repository, 1885.

Delitzsch, Franz. *A System of Biblical Psychology.* Edinburgh: T. & T. Clark, 1890. Pp. 337-360.

_____. *Biblical Commentary on the Prophecies of Isaiah.* Vol. 2. Edinburgh: T. & T. Clark, 1892.

Demon Experiences in Many Lands. A compilation. Chicago: Moody Press, 1960, Pp. 92-95.

Douglas, W. M. *Andrew Murray and His Message.* London: Oliphants, n.d. Pp. 180-201.

Fant, D. J. *Modern Miracles of Healing.* Harrisburg, Pa.: Christian Publications, 1943.

Farr, Fredrick W. *A Manual of Christian Doctrine.* New York: Alliance Press, n.d.

Fowler, Charles J. *Thoughts on Prayer.* Chicago: Christian Witness Co., 1912. Pp. 88-112.

Frazier, Claude A. *Faith Healing, Finger of God? or Scientific Curiosity?* New York: Thomas Nelson, 1973.

Frost, Evelyn. *Christian Healing.* London: A. R. Mowbray & Co., 1940.

Frost, Henry W. *Miraculous Healing.* Westwood, N.J.: Fleming H. Revell, 1952.

Goforth, Jonathan. *By My Spirit.* Reprint. Minneapolis: Bethany Fellowship, 1964.

Gordon, A. J. *The Ministry of Healing.* 1882 Reprint. Harrisburg, Pa.: Christian Publications, n.d.

Gordon, S. D. *Quiet Talks About the Healing Christ.* New York: Fleming H. Revell, 1924.

Green, Michael. *Evangelism in the Early Church.* Grand Rapids, Mich.: Wm. B. Eerdmans Publishing Co., 1970.

Guest, W. *Pastor Blumhardt and His Work.* London: Morgan & Scott, 1881.

Harris, Douglas J. *The Biblical Concept of Peace, Shalom.* Grand Rapids, Mich.: Baker Book House, 1970.

Hegre, T. A. *The Cross and Sanctification.* Minneapolis: Bethany Fellowship, 1963. Pp. 219-246.

Hodge, Archibald A. *The Atonement.* Reprint. Grand Rapids, Mich.: Baker Book House, 1974.

Hoyt, Herman A. *All Things Whatsoever I Have Commanded You.* Winona Lake, Ind.: Brethren Press, 1948. Pp. 36-54.

Jacobus, Melancthon W. *Notes on the Gospels.* New York: Robert Carter & Bros., 1857.

Kennedy, Mrs. H. H. *Victor Lombard of Geneva.* New York: Alliance Press Co., 1906.

Kirby, Gilbert W. *The Question of Healing.* London: Victory Press, 1967.

Koch, Kurt E. *Between Christ and Satan.* Grand Rapids, Mich.: Kregel, 1961. Pp. 183-199.

Lenski, R. C. H. *The Interpretation of St. Paul's First and Second Epistles to the Corinthians.* Columbus, Ohio: Wartburg Press, 1946.

Leupold, H. C. *Exposition of Genesis.* Columbus, Ohio: Wartburg Press, 1942.

_____. *Exposition of Genesis.* Vol. 2. Grand Rapids, Mich.: Baker Book House, 1959.

McCrossan, T. J. *Bodily Healing and the Atonement.* Seattle: McCrosson Publishers, 1930.

MacKenzie, Kenneth. *Divine Life for the Body.* New York: Christian Alliance Publishing Co., 1926.

_____. *Our Physical Heritage.* New York: Fleming H. Revell, 1923.

MacMillan, J. A. *Modern Demon Possession.* Harrisburg, Pa.: Christian Publications, n.d.

Marsh, F. E. *Emblems of the Holy Spirit.* Reprint. Fincastle, Va.: Scripture Truth Book Co., 1967. Pp. 85-86.

Marsh, R. L. *Faith Healing: A Defense.* Chicago: Fleming H. Revell, 1889.

Marshall, Catherine. *Beyond Ourselves.* New York: McGraw-Hill Book Co., 1961. Pp., 199-226.

Mauro, Philip. *Sickness Among Saints.* Boston: Hamilton Bros., 1909.

Modersohn, Ernst. *Men of Revival in Germany.* Frankfurt: Herolds Publishers, 1970.

Monsen, Marie. *The Awakening: Revival in China, a Work of the Holy Spirit.* London: China Inland Mission, 1959.

Murray, Andrew. *Divine Healing.* 1900. Reprint. Fort Washington, Pa.: Christian Literature Crusade, n.d.

Nee, Watchman. *The Spiritual Man.* Vol. 3. New York: Christian Fellowship Publisher, 1968. Pp. 139-212.

Nevius, John L. *Demon Possession.* 1894. Reprint. Grand Rapids, Mich.: Kregel Publications, 1968.

Oerter, J. H. *Divine Healing in the Light of Scripture.* Brooklyn, N.Y.: Christian Alliance Publishing Co., 1900.

Olsen, Peder. *Healing Through Prayer.* Minneapolis: Augsburg Publishing House, 1962.

Pastor Blumhardt. New York: Christian Alliance Publishing Co., n.d.

Patton, William. *Prayer and Its Remarkable Answers.* Cleveland: Lauer & Mattil, 1892.

235

Peak, Giles M. *Christ's Healing Wings*. New York, Christian Alliance Publishing Co., 1900.

Penn-Lewis, Jessie. *All Things New*. Bournemouth: Overcomer Book Room, 1931. Pp. 70-78.

Penn-Lewis, Jessie, and Roberts, Evan. *War on the Saints*. Bournemouth: Overcomer Book Room, 1912.

Pentecost, J. Dwight. *Things to Come: A Study in Biblical Eschatology*. Findlay, Ohio: Dunham Publishing Co., 1958.

Peters, George W. *Saturation Evangelism*. Grand Rapids, Mich.: Zondervan Publishing House, 1970.

Pierson, Arthur T. *George Müller of Bristol*. 1899. Reprint. New York: Fleming H. Revell Co., n.d.

_____. *The New Acts of the Apostles*. New York: Baker & Taylor Co., 1894.

Pink, Arthur W. *Divine Healing*. Swengel, Pa.: Reiner Publications, n.d.

Pitts, John. *Divine Healing, Fact or Fiction*. Evesham: Arthur James, 1962.

Pridie, J. R. *The Church's Ministry of Healing*. London: Society for Promoting Christian Knowledge, 1926.

Pullan, Leighton. *Early Christian Doctrine*. New York: Edwin S. Gorham, 1905. Pp. 72-86.

Puller, F. W. *The Anointing of the Sick*. London: Society for Promoting Christian Knowledge, 1904.

Ramm, Bernard. *The Pattern of Authority*. Grand Rapids, Mich.: Wm. B. Eerdmans Publishing Co., 1957.

Rice, John R. *Prayer—Asking and Receiving*. Wheaton, Ill.: Sword of the Lord Publishers, 1942. Pp. 96-126.

Riley, W. B. *Divine Healing, or Does God Answer Prayer for the Sick?* New York: Christian Alliance Publishing Co., 1899.

Ringenberg, J. A. *Jesus the Healer*. Fort Wayne, Ind.: Missionary Church Association, 1947.

Rite of Anointing and Pastoral Care of the Sick. New York: Catholic Book Publishing Co., 1974.

Roberts, Alexander, and Donaldson, James, eds. *The Ante-Nicene Fathers*. 10 vols. 1867. Reprint. Grand Rapids, Mich.: Wm. B. Eerdmans Publishing Co., 1951.

Scharpff, Paulus. *The History of Evangelism.* Grand Rapids, Mich.: Wm. B. Eerdmans Publishing Co., 1966.

Shaw, S. B. *Touching Incidents and Remarkable Answers to Prayer.* Cincinnati: M. W. Knapp, 1897.

Short, A. Rendle. *The Bible and Modern Medicine.* Chicago: Moody Press, 1967.

Short, J. N. *Divine Healing.* Chicago: Christian Witness Co., n.d.

Shrier, Clarence. *The God of Health.* Harrisburg, Pa.: Christian Publications, 1968.

Simpson, A. B. *First Corinthians: The Principles and Life of the Apostolic Church.* Christ in the Bible Series, vol. 18. Harrisburg, Pa.: Christian Publications, n.d.

_____. *Friday Meeting Talks.* 3 vols. New York: Christian Alliance Publishing Co.; vol. 1, 1894; vol. 2, 1899; vol. 3, 1900.

_____. *Inquiries and Answers.* New York: Word, Work, & World Publishing Co., 1887.

_____. *Life of Christ.* Christ in the Bible Series, vol. 8. New York: Word, Work, & World Publishing Co., 1888.

_____. *Present Truths or the Supernatural.* Reprint. Harrisburg, Pa.: Christian Publications, n.d. Pp. 53-67.

_____. *The Gospel of Healing.* Harrisburg, Pa.: Christian Publications, 1915.

_____. *The Lord for the Body.* New York: Christian Alliance Publishing Co., 1925.

_____. *The Old Faith and the New Gospel.* Reprint. Harrisburg, Pa.: Christian Publications, n.d. Pp. 58-67.

_____. *Walking in the Spirit.* Reprint. Harrisburg, Pa.: Christian Publications, n.d. Pp. 61-74.

Smith, Jennie. *From Baca to Beulah.* Philadelphia: Garrigues Bros., 1889. Pp. 354-355.

Smith, Oswald J. *The Great Physician.* New York: Christian Alliance Publishing Co., 1927.

Snead, A. C. *The Eternal Christ.* Published by the author, 1936. Pp. 46-50.

Spurgeon, C. H. *The Metropolitan Pulpit.* Vol. 28. London: Passmore & Alabaster, 1882.

Stanton, R. L. *Gospel Parallelisms, Healing of Body and Soul.* Buffalo, N.Y.: Triumph of Faith, 1884.

Stevens, W. C. *Revelation, the Crown Jewel of Prophecy.* Vol. 1. New York: Christian Alliance Publishing Co., 1928. Pp. 406-439.

Straton, John Roach. *Divine Healing in Scripture and Life.* New York: Christian Alliance Publishing Co., 1927.

Torrey, Reuben A. *Divine Healing.* Reprint. Chicago: Moody Press, n.d.

Trench, Richard C. *Notes on the Miracles of Our Lord.* London: Macmillan & Co., 1878.

Uttley, Frank. *The Supreme Physician.* London: James Clark & Co., 1950.

Vollmer, Philip. *Modern Students' Life of Christ.* New York: Fleming H. Revell, 1912.

Warfield, Benjamin B. *Miracles Yesterday and Today.* Reprint of *Counterfeit Miracles,* 1918. Grand Rapids, Mich.: Wm. B. Eerdmans Publishing Co., 1965.

Watson, George D. *Holiness Manual.* Cincinnati: God's Revivalist Press, 1898. Pp. 141-144.

Wetherill, Francis M. *Healing in the Churches.* New York: Fleming H. Revell, 1925.

Wheatly, Charles. *A Rational Illustration of the Book of Common Prayer.* Oxford: University Press, 1839. Pp. 418-454.

Whittle, D. W. *The Wonders of Prayer.* New York: Fleming H. Revell, 1885.

Wilcox, Vernon L. *God's Healing Touch.* Kansas City, Mo.: Beacon Hill Press, 1968.

Wilson, Henry B. *The Revival of the Gift of Healing.* London: Young Churchman Co., 1914.

_____. *Does Christ Still Heal?* New York: E. P. Dutton & Co., 1917.

Wilson, Robert N. *Medical Men in the Time of Christ.* Philadelphia: Sunday School Times, 1912.